EARLY
GERMANIC KINGSHIP

EARLY
GERMANIC KINGSHIP
IN ENGLAND AND ON
THE CONTINENT

*The Ford Lectures
delivered in the University of Oxford
in Hilary Term 1970*

by

J. M. WALLACE-HADRILL

FELLOW OF MERTON COLLEGE, OXFORD
AND OF THE BRITISH ACADEMY

OXFORD
AT THE CLARENDON PRESS
1971

Oxford University Press, Ely House, London W.1

GLASGOW NEW YORK TORONTO MELBOURNE WELLINGTON
CAPE TOWN SALISBURY IBADAN NAIROBI DAR ES SALAAM LUSAKA ADDIS ABABA
BOMBAY CALCUTTA MADRAS KARACHI LAHORE DACCA
KUALA LUMPUR SINGAPORE HONG KONG TOKYO

PRINTED IN GREAT BRITAIN

TO
CORPUS CHRISTI COLLEGE
OXFORD

PREFACE

It would be possible to write a big book about Anglo-Saxon kingship, and an even larger one about continental kingship. All I have attempted in these six lectures—which I publish, with slight alterations, as I delivered them—is to draw attention to some common strands in thought and action that tend to bring English and continental history a little nearer together in one field. I endeavour to relate early medieval thinking about kingship to the practice of kings. Between what kings did and what others thought they should be doing there lies a gulf; but, as I see it, the gulf is not so wide nor so insurmountable as at first it looks. It is not a matter to which English historians have ever paid much attention. But the situation is quite otherwise on the continent. I could, and perhaps should, have filled my footnotes with a huge continental literature, but refrained. Many foreign scholars, among whom I number several good friends, have recently published important work without which I should have made a poor showing: I may instance the writings of Professor Eugen Ewig, of Bonn. I owe them much more than my acknowledgements in the footnotes would suggest. One English historian, Professor Walter Ullmann, of Cambridge, is indeed the author of a remarkable book that touches closely on the matter of my two concluding lectures. No one who is interested in the subject can afford to neglect his *Carolingian Renaissance and the Idea of Kingship*, which appeared when my book was almost complete. Our approach is rather different but we move in the same world.

Several English colleagues have helped me in fields where they are more expert than I. Specifically I should like to thank Professor A. Momigliano, Dr. J. N. L. Myres, and Dr. R. L. S. Bruce-Mitford, all of whom read chapters in draft and saved me in the way that scholars do save each other. Even greater, however, is my debt, scholarly and other, to my wife. While I have been writing, I have often wondered what two former Ford's

PREFACE

Lecturers, Sir Maurice Powicke and Professor Wilhelm Levison,
would have made of it. I remember one of them with affection,
and both gratefully.

J. M. W-H.

Merton College, Oxford

CONTENTS

I

GERMANIC KINGSHIP AND THE ROMANS

WHAT evidence can we use to form an idea of the beginnings of Germanic kingship? There is a proto-Germanic history into which archaeology and shreds of tradition allow us some insights. They could scarcely be expected to allow us more. Certainly they do not reach to a matter so specific as the origins of kingship. We cannot define it in terms of, say, the Germans of the first century B.C.; we do not know what word or words they used to describe their kings; we do not know what those kings were for. We may assume their existence, and that is as far as we should go. It may be that the Scandinavian sagas and laws conceal a wealth of detail for these early times; many good scholars have thought so; but I should not care to use them in any but a supporting role.[1] For facts we must wait till the Romans speak. How far was a Roman historian able to understand the Germanic practice of kingship? Could he, for example, recognize what is nowadays called the sacral element in Germanic kingship when he chanced upon it? Could he be expected to assume its existence? Like the Greeks, the Romans had been pretty thorough in reducing their own kings to sacral functions and kept a reasonably clear record of the operation.[2] Their historians knew very well that kings had to perform religious functions even when they were no longer performing political or military ones. They were sensitive to the religious aspects of kingship, whether at home or abroad. Thus, when we turn to Tacitus, a vital if Delphic Roman witness of Germanic kingship, we can assume that he had a clear idea of what kingship had meant and ought to mean to Romans. There was no need to spell it out to Roman readers.

[1] See Claudio Albani, *L'istituto monachico nell'antica società nordica* (Florence, 1969), especially on law.
[2] For the Romans, see A. Momigliano, 'Il Rex Sacrorum e l'origine della Republica', in *Studi in onore di Edoardo Volterra*, i (1969).

The occasion of the writing of the *Germania* is not in doubt:[3] Trajan stood upon the banks of the Rhine, face to face with a problem that the Empire had never solved and never was to solve: how to deal with Germans; how to contain them; how to subjugate them; and how, if possible, to make them love Romans without being loved in return. It was a chance for a fresh start. All this Tacitus grasped. He saw, too, a point traditionally dear to Roman intellectuals: that their own political troubles were a consequence of moral decline. How better to drive this home than by fathering lost Roman virtues on the poor barbarians? So Tacitus took down from his shelves the elder Pliny's *Bella Germaniae*, and with the help of this and other books composed a famous monograph. The *Germania* is not like any other of Tacitus' books. It is not concerned with the great theme of Germanic liberty. It does not idealize the Germans or their habits. It is critical of their lack of courage and toughness, their lack of energy and purpose in peacetime, their drunkenness and gambling, their agriculture and housing, their revolting size. It gives no good marks to their political organization. What is approved are precisely those virtues that the Romans were believed to have lost: predominantly the family virtues, chastity first among them; and that was all. Whether or not Tacitus had ever visited the Rhine frontier, he felt no need to consult those who had. He knew what he had to say, and the material to hand enabled him to say it. It amounts to this: the *Germania* is not only an unsafe guide to future Germanic society, it also affords no solid ground for generalization about Germanic society at large of the historian's own time. It describes the ways of certain Germans, how exactly we cannot tell, at a particular and altogether exceptional moment in their history. One consolation we have is that Tacitus was ever careful in his choice of words. He says that his Germans had *reges*. *Rex* was an ancient and curious word. Its stem was cognate with the Sanskrit, which was also the ancestor of the Celtic word **rigs*, from which in turn all the Germanic languages borrowed it.[4] What was the characteris-

---

[3] See R. Syme, *Tacitus*, i (1958), pp. 46, 126–7; A. N. Sherwin-White, *Racial Prejudice in Imperial Rome* (1967), ch. 2.

[4] For a wider discussion of the word and its possible sacral overtones in primitive times, see D. A. Binchy, *Celtic and Anglo-Saxon Kingship* (O'Donnell Lectures, Oxford, 1970), pp. 3, 4.

tic of the Tacitean *rex*? It was *nobilitas*. For this, says Tacitus, *reges* were 'taken' by the Germans: 'reges ex nobilitate ... sumunt.'[5] He used a semantically neutral verb, *sumere*, that implied nothing about how the taking was managed. In this respect they differed from certain war-leaders whom he calls *duces:* these were 'taken' for *virtus*, prowess in the field. He does not say that *reges* could not be *duces*, but only that they owed their position, whatever it entailed, to a different quality. He adds that their authority was not absolute— absolute, that is, in the sense in which a Roman would understand it; further, that the attention commanded by a *rex* or *princeps* in a Germanic assembly bore some relation to his age, birth, military prestige, or eloquence; that part of the fine imposed on culprits went to the *rex*; and that freedmen were rated low except possibly among peoples who had *reges*. It is with the *princeps* that Tacitus associates the *comitatus* or sworn war-band: he is rather more like a *dux* than a *rex*. Tacitus' idea of the Germanic *rex* is more of a tribal leader than a warrior or a priest. We cannot be sure what he does, except that he speaks in assemblies, receives fines, and knows how to use freedmen. It is possible for a people to do without him. We cannot be sure that he has, or need have in Roman eyes, any of the virtues proper to a ruler of civilized men. One cannot imagine any Roman writer, from Tacitus to Claudian, discovering in a Germanic king the imperial qualities that Theodosius recommended to his son.[6] Yet these same Romans, in non-Germanic contexts, were clear that the mere name of *rex* implied a moral content: a king should be able to rule himself as well as others. Thus Cicero dismisses Tarquin, 'qui nec se nec suos regere potuit';[7] Horace refers to a child's game with its refrain 'rex eris ... si recte facies';[8] and in the *Disticha Catonis* we find 'Tu si animo regeris, rex es, si corpore, servus'.[9] Here was one source from which early medieval writers, from Cassiodorus to Gregory the Great, Isidore, and beyond, were to take the seminal idea of public rule being conditional upon self-rule.[10] It is not in the

[5] *Germania*, ch. 7.
[6] Claudian, *De Quarto Consulatu Honorii*, vv. 219-27, 266, 276, 294, 299, 303.
[7] *De Finibus Bonorum et Malorum*, iii. 75. See also *De Re Publ.* ii. 3. i.
[8] *Epistulae*, I. i. 57 ff.   [9] *Poetae Latini Minores*, iii, p. 237.
[10] For this see H. H. Anton, *Fürstenspiegel und Herrscherethos in der Karolingerzeit* (Bonn, 1968), pp. 384-5.

Roman historians, however. But if they do not suggest that the Germanic kings knew anything about self-rule, it does not follow that such kings as dealt familiarly with Romans did not carry notions of this sort home with them.

For a time, the Germans among whom these kings existed appeared to the Romans as a uniform mass, different from the Celts, very different from themselves. But it was to Celtic and Roman influence that they owed much of what distinguished them politically from their ancestors and made them, by the end of the first century, anything but an undifferentiated mass.[11] Tacitus' Germans were not those of Caesar a century earlier, nor those of Ammianus and Procopius in the centuries that followed. Greek and Roman writers differed about what they saw because what they saw was different. The Celtic tribes, among whom many of the more westerly German peoples had lived for generations, had given them much of political organization. This may have included the war-band, bound by oaths to its leader, whom to survive in battle was deepest dishonour.[12] Of war-bands in general, so characteristic of the Germans, it is necessary to say this: that the *comitatus* carefully described by Tacitus was something rather specialized. It was a company of freeborn warriors sworn to help their lord in peace as well as war. One can imagine that its upkeep in peacetime might well be a heavy charge;[13] heavy enough to discourage many chieftains from permanent dependence on that particular kind of war-band. For there were other kinds of war-band; for example, the servile attendants of a warrior's household, often numerous enough to constitute a field force, and war-bands specially raised for temporary needs and then disbanded. Servile status and temporary service are

[11] Dr. C. M. Wells, reviewing R. Nierhaus, *Das swebische Gräberfeld von Diersheim* (Berlin, 1966) in *J.R.S.* lix (1969), pp. 303–5, points out that it becomes increasingly difficult, if not impossible, to distinguish Germans from Celts archaeologically in the first century B.C. and to get behind Caesar's (and so Tacitus') geographical definition of Gauls and Germans, which took small account of ethnography. The Celtic element in continental Germanic kingship may thus be greater than we suppose; but I see no means of assessing how much greater.

[12] R. Wenskus, *Stammesbildung und Verfassung* (Cologne–Graz, 1961), p. 357 and *passim* for a full assessment of the Germans' debt to the Celts.

[13] See Hans Kuhn, 'Die Grenzen der germanischen Gefolgschaft', *Zeitsch. der Savigny Stift., Germ. Abt.* lxxiii (1956), pp. 4, 5.

sometimes found among later Germanic war-bands. Which of these forms will have originated in the Germanic past and which as a result of contact with the Romano-Celtic world, we cannot now say. One should think twice before maintaining that the *comitatus* Tacitus described was the only kind of war-band known to the Germans, or that they invented it.

The Germans knew the Romans both as implacable enemies and as useful employers, and had so known them before the time of Tacitus. It is not surprising, then, that Roman writers should sometimes, if without much regard for niceties of rank, have recorded the doings of Germanic chieftains of one kind or another. Tacitus himself, in his *Histories* and *Annals,* though mainly in the special context of their love of liberty, has a good deal to say about them. Four such early leaders deserve attention.[14] First, there was Ariovistus, described by Caesar as *rex Germanorum* and acknowledged as *rex* by the Senate.[15] He commanded a medley of Germanic followings in arms and dealt personally with the Romans on questions of hostages, tribute, and the lands of his subject Celts in Gaul. His aim was land-acquisition, not for a single *gens* but for all those who had left their homes for good and followed him to war. None the less, he achieved *amicitia* of a sort with the Romans: *rex* described him best. We do not know if he was of ancient royal blood. Before a critical battle he consulted the oracles, the *matres familiae,* though when it came to the point he took no notice of what they said.[16] Also, he took two wives, one a German and the other a non-German princess: polygamy was often to be practised in families of Germanic kings. Secondly, there was Maroboduus, another Germanic war-leader who in Roman eyes enjoyed *certum imperium* and *vis regia;*[17] for he overthrew neighbouring tribes, and break-away groups as well as prominent enemies of Rome flocked to him. Tacitus calls him *rex* of the Suebi,[18] and refers to his royal headquarters and his treasure. Like Ariovistus,

[14] On what follows see the valuable study of Walter Schlesinger, 'Das Heerkönigtum', in *Das Königtum, seine geistigen und rechtlichen Grundlagen* (Lindau–Konstanz, 1956), pp. 116–21.

[15] *De Bello Gallico,* i. 43.

[16] Ibid. i. 44.

[17] Velleius Paterculus, *Historiae Romanae,* ii, ch. 108.

[18] *Annals,* ii. 26, 62.

he was ruler of whatever men were induced to join him from dis-affection or hope of land. Defeated in the end, he saw his follow-ing disintegrate. Even so, he seems to have established a *stirps regia*, for Tacitus had heard of kings belonging to it among the Marcomanni.[19] According to Velleius Paterculus he was of dis-tinguished blood, *genere nobilis*, which could be a way of saying royal blood.[20] Thirdly, we have Arminius, conqueror of Maro-boduus. For twelve years he exercised *potentia*[21] without ever calling himself king, for he took note of the unpopularity of Maroboduus, who had done so. He preferred to be thought of as a fighter for freedom.[22] He was remembered in song,[23] and his nephew, Italicus, who lived in Rome, was said to belong to a *stirps regia*.[24] To the Romans at least Arminius was a king, even if his own followers disliked the implications. He seems not to have fought with the aim of land acquisition, like Ariovistus and Maroboduus, nor to have led, as they did, loose followings of many peoples. He led whole *gentes* and his aim was liberation from Rome. Of his background we know nothing. It may, then, be that we are looking at leaders engaged in two kinds of Ger-manic warfare: the war of a *gens* or of united *gentes* for freedom, and that of large war-bands for new land.[25] In the former, some restraint may have been placed on the leader's authority; in the latter, none. A *gens* fighting for survival will naturally feel that there is something sacral about its cause; hence, it may give special authority to its priesthood and sacrifice prisoners to the gods. However, something like this authority is also discernible in the wars of a fourth Germanic commander, Julius Civilis, who certainly did not lead united *gentes* in a fight for freedom but belonged rather to the other type of war-leader. Civilis was a Batavian of royal blood[26] and came of a family that had some claim to Roman education. Gauls as well as Germans followed him when he went to war in a Roman province. He seems to have undergone a form of initiation as a commander, *barbaro ritu*; for he took an oath. With this, human sacrifice and ritual dancing were associated. It would not be surprising if, like Brinnus,

[19] *Germania*, ch. 42.
[20] *Hist. Rom.* ii. ch. 108.
[21] Tacitus, *Annals*, ii. 88.
[22] Ibid. ii. 44.
[23] Ibid. ii. 88.
[24] Ibid. xi. 16.
[25] This view is developed by Schlesinger, pp. 119 ff.
[26] Tacitus, *Hist.* iv. 13.

he was also raised on a war-shield. Furthermore, Civilis grew his hair long and dyed it red, keeping it thus for the length of his war with the Romans. Royal blood was not enough: more was required to make him a commander of the right type. For a time at least, he seems to have owed his authority to a form of special election.

These four leaders had something in common. Whatever kind of barbarian confederation formed round them, and whatever their own backgrounds, they exercised a power for which Rome had a word: it was kingly. What impressed Rome about power of this kind was that those who had it could negotiate and treat with Roman officials with some hope that their followers would accept their decisions; they were rather more than warrior-chieftains of an older pattern. A *rex* knew his Romans even when he fought them. He did not need to be a *magister militum* in Roman pay or serve in Roman camps and courts, as other Germans were soon to do,[27] to learn that contact with Rome altered your relations with your own followers. This was true in peace as in war; and by Tacitus' time the Germans on the Rhine had found a temporary stability that for them amounted to peace. It has been argued[28] that the Romans associated kings with sacral leadership of entire *gentes*, not with warrior con-federations. To begin with, this may have been true; and what the Romans thought will in turn have influenced the Germans' outlook on their own leadership.[29] In the first century we are only at the beginning of Roman influence on Germanic kingship.[30]

Kings, then, whatever they did, were useful to Romans and Germans alike, if in different ways. When we move into the

---

[27] For whom consult especially K. F. Stroheker, 'Zur Rolle der Heermeister fränkischer Abstammung im späten vierten Jahrhundert', reprinted in *Germanentum und Spätantike* (Zürich–Stuttgart, 1965).

[28] By Schlesinger, p. 110.

[29] Kuhn, pp. 9, 54, 57, 78, holds that the Romans taught the Germans oath-taking, protection, and vassalage.

[30] Two respects in which there may have been early influence were (i) that of Roman *protectores* on the development of the *comitatus* (O. Seeck, 'Das deutsche Gefolgswesen auf römischen Boden', *Zeitsch. der Sav. Stift., Germ. Abt.* xvii (1896), pp. 98–118) and (ii) that of gladiators on the emergence of Germanic champions who engaged in single combat for their people (cf. Kuhn, p. 68).

fourth and fifth centuries we find more of them. Yet they were still no essential part of Germanic society. Some Germans did without kings, as, for example, the Saxons, the Gepids, and, for a while, the Herules, who were rather old-fashioned in more ways than one: they even sent back to Scandinavia for a new king of the right dynasty, and found there no shortage of qualified candidates.[31] Other Germans dispensed with kings from time to time, while continuing to recognize the existence of royal blood. The kings we do have, however, were very powerful men, *conquistadores* whose careers reveal that kingship had not stood still. Modern German scholarship likes to classify them as *Grosskönige, Heerkönige*, and *Kleinkönige*;[32] which is as much as to say that some kings were more powerful than others. It can mark no distinction between the quality of one king and another, and possibly there was none. I therefore make no use of these classifications.

In Scandinavia the Germans worshipped their own pantheon: Tiwaz, Thor, Frey, Odin (or Woden), and plenty more. Nor did they forget them when they migrated south. In contact with Celts and Romans, some of these gods acquired new names and fresh attributes. Woden, for instance, could be identified with Mercury, Thor with Jupiter. Roman and Germanic paganism were not antipathetic. As in Scandinavia so within the Empire, kings without being priests could link the gods with those they ruled; they could appease and placate the gods and be deposed in sacrificial propitiation when things went wrong. The kings of the migrating Germans, like those of the Scandinavians, were sacral, by which we mean that they were cult-kings, representing the moral lives and domestic ideals of their people, incapsulating good luck. The old Scandinavian kings were certainly not thought to be descended from the gods or indeed to have a dynastic right to rule; but movement and victory and contact with Rome somehow changed this for the continental Germanic kings, who came to feel that there was something god-like in them, whether through association in office or through descent. A commonplace of later Germanic tradition was to be the royal genealogy that derived a dynasty from a particular god, though when this

---

[31] See Wenskus, p. 431; Procopius, *Hist.* vi. xv. 27–30.
[32] e.g. Schlesinger, art. cit.

started is anyone's guess. Conversion to Christianity did nothing
to weaken belief, or at least interest, in descent from the gods,
whether descent of peoples or of kings. Indeed, it may have done
something to strengthen it: the sacred character of Christian kingship could be read back into the past. Let me take an example.
The Christianity that fell to the lot of the East German peoples
happened to be Arianism; and it came to them later and more
slowly, perhaps, than was once believed. Arianism and paganism
long continued to co-exist. It was to the chieftains that the Arian
missionaries most effectively addressed themselves, not to those
they led. Of the East Germans in question—Goths, Vandals,
Lombards, and Burgundians—the sources tell us most about the
conversion of the Goths. It began in the mid-fourth century
with the mission of Bishop Ulfila to a small group of Visigoths
in the Black Sea area. Yet when the Visigoths reached Moesia in
382 most of them were still pagan. Between that date and 395
the Christian minority became a majority, perhaps because the
wretched conditions under which they lived discredited the
pagan gods, perhaps also because a rising nobility of Visigoth
landowners and chieftains had reached that stage when it was
natural to ape their Roman counterparts and try Christianity.
One can imagine that Arianism made a special appeal to those
in authority, with its insistence on a hierarchized Trinity informed by obedience and conceived in strictly anthropomorphic
terms.[33] The Ostrogothic confederation that reached Italy under
Theodoric's kingship were for the most part Arian. Yet they
had not forgotten the pagan past. The Theodoric we know
from the *Variae* of Cassiodorus and from Ennodius is a ruler
of Romans devout in the service of *Romanitas*; the Theodoric
his Gothic followers knew was a Germanic war-leader and a very
different kind of man. This we can infer from the factual residue
in the medieval legends of Dietrich of Bern. We know it also
from a famous inscription on the Rökstone, from ninth-century
Scandinavia.[34] Varin the rune-master dedicates his son to

---

[33] See E. A. Thompson, *The Visigoths in the Time of Ulfila* (1966), p. 109 and
passim. On Ulfila as a Christian pacifist, anxious to play down the warlike
spirit of the Goths, see D. H. Green, *The Carolingian Lord* (1965), p. 279.
[34] The interpretation of this much-disputed inscription which I here follow
is that of Otto Höfler, *Germanisches Sakralkönigtum*, i (Münster, 1952), *Der
Runenstein von Rök und die germanische Individualweihe*.

Theodoric in expectation of vengeance for the death of another son, Vemod, at the hands of twenty sea-kings. This was more than legend it was active religious belief. The inscription also testifies that Theodoric had been dead for nine generations; once a king, he now sits armed on his horse. The rune-master will perhaps have been identifying him with Woden as victory-giver. The Scandinavians in Gotland (the stone is in Östergötland) have continued to feel kinship with the Goths in Italy and have remembered Theodoric, last of the great Gothic kings. What is more, they know of him as a sea-king. The ninth-century Vikings would no doubt think thus of a king in any case, but it just so happens that one of the last acts of Theodoric recorded by Cassiodorus is that he built an Adriatic fleet of a thousand ships in the port of Ravenna.[35] In brief, the Vikings thought of Theodoric as a sacral king: it would not follow that the Ostrogoths did, nine generations earlier. But there is more evidence. Their historian, Jordanes, asserts that the Goths looked upon the Amal dynasty (from which Theodoric wrongly but necessarily claimed descent) as *semi-dei*.[36] I find it hard to believe that Jordanes (and still less Cassiodorus) would have invented a king-saga to persuade the Romans of Gothic respectability (though it may have done this) unless the material of the saga first made sense to the Goths. At the head of the Gothic genealogy, which Jordanes recites, stands the hero Gapt. Gapt or Gaut also figures in Scandinavian mythology as an emanation or incarnation of Odin[37] and as the eponymous founder of another, related people, the Gautar. To Odin I shall presently return. For the moment it is enough to note that not only the Scandinavians but equally the Ostrogoths regarded Theodoric and his dynasty as kings of divine descent in whom divinity was active for the good of the people. He was no stay-at-home king of peace, such as H. M. Chadwick long ago distinguished for his sacral role from the adventuring war-band leader of Germanic Europe.[38] He was one

[35] *Variae*, v. xvi ff.
[36] *Getica*, xiii. 76 ff. See also v. 40–1, 48, and xi. 71 for further stories of the royal Gothic past.
[37] O. Höfler, 'Der Sakralcharakter des germanischen Königtums', in *Das Königtum*, pp. 95–6. See now K. Hauck, *Goldbrakteaten aus Sievern* (Munich, 1970), *s.v.* 'Gaut', 'Hathugaut'.
[38] *The Heroic Age* (1926), p. 377.

of the most successful of all war-band leaders, under whom a very
large confederation of Goths and others settled in Italy. Yet
Jordanes means his readers to understand that his sacral role
was real enough and was derived from his ancestry, not from
his conquests. Those conquests or accessions of power were
indeed marked at three stages by what look like special initia-
tions.[39] With each, as fresh war-bands joined him, he felt the
need to submit to a ceremony of initiation for the benefit of the
newcomers, when they could acknowledge him as their war-
leader; possibly also as something more. For the fighters were
accompanied by their families, which means that many of the
Germans who reached Italy were not warriors at all but women
and children, dependants and slaves. Tacitus himself bore witness that the Germanic wife was expected to be her husband's
companion in war as well as peace. Using the term loosely,
Theodoric was head of a great *comitatus*; at the same time he
was king of a people and of subjected peoples. War-bands are
tribes in the making. It may be that Theodoric's roles were less
clearly demarcated for his barbarian contemporaries than they
are for us. What worried them was not what sort of a Germanic
leader he was but whether he were not more of a Roman official.
It was *Romanitas* that discredited his dynasty in the end. With
the destruction of their kingship by Justinian the Goths too dis-
appeared as a people. Gibbon was right to see the end of King
Totila as a kind of *Götterdämmerung*.[40]

The story of the kingship of the Vandals is not essentially
different.[41] Like the Goths, the Vandals were primarily a *gens*,
one people, to which from time to time others attached themselves. These would not all have been Germans; Celtic influence
was strong among them. Their two main divisions bore the
names of the royal dynasties under whom they rose to prominence: Hasdings and Silings. The Hasding Vandals first emerge
in A.D. 171 under two kings, Raus and Rapt, enemies of Rome.[42]

[39] On which see Wenskus, *Stammesbildung*, pp. 482 ff.

[40] *Decline and Fall*, iv, pp. 203–4. Hanno Helbling, *Goten und Wandalen*
(Zürich, 1954), pp. 59 ff., discusses changing views on Gothic kingship.

[41] It is best treated by Christian Courtois, *Les Vandales et l'Afrique* (Paris,
1955), pp. 16–50, 245–8.

[42] Dio Cassius, *Hist.*, lxxi. 12. 1. For Raus and Rapt as possible cult-names,
see Mrs. J. E. Turville-Petre, 'Hengest and Horsa', *Saga-Book of the Viking
Society*, xiv, pt. 4 (1956–7), pp. 276–7.

They could fight, therefore, though they were a sedentary agricultural people like the Goths, with a mediocre domestic skill in metalwork and pottery. Their eruption into Gaul in 406 was the result of sudden coalition under national kings into a military confederation that carried all before it. Yet the confederation broke up as rapidly as it had arisen, for in a few months the Vandals and their friends were scattered, and a few years after that, some were still in Gaul,[43] more were in Spain, and most in Africa. The confederation was scattered; kings remained. The successful military background of the royal dynasty told against it in more peaceful times in Africa, when men recalled the days of war, though they now lived under kings who were no longer, or not enough, interested in fighting. How could a king go on claiming exceptional authority, such as sprang from war-leadership, when, like Hilderic, he detested any mention of military affairs?[44] His situation was altogether too like that of a certain Herule king who had played draughts during a battle.[45] The destruction of the Vandal kings in war, again by Justinian's generals, also caused the disappearance of the people. Whatever Vandal kingship had been, the Vandals themselves were identified with it in war and peace. And peace was the problem for kings.

A little more can be said about the sacral content of kingship such as we have detected in the Goths and can imagine in the Vandals. It is often associated with the cult of Woden,[46] who seemed to be a favourite god with war-bands. Scandinavian mythology connected him with a wide assortment of activities: harvest, poetry, love-ventures, magic, trickery, storm, human sacrifice, death in battle, and fury. 'Wodan, id est furor', was Adam of Bremen's opinion,[47] some time later. The demoniac and the wild man in him were quite uncharacteristic of gods like Thor and Frey, both of whom were attractive to kings. Frey, the fertility god, was a special favourite, and it cannot be chance

---

[43] Their movements there are described by Bernard S. Bachrach, 'The Alans in Gaul', *Traditio*, xxiii (1967).

[44] Procopius, *Hist.* I. IX. I.

[45] Paulus Diaconus, *Hist. Langobardorum*, i. 20.

[46] See O. Höfler, *Kultische Geheimbünde der Germanen* (Frankfurt, 1934), pp. 324–38.

[47] *Gesta Hammaburgensis Eccl. Pont.* iv, ch. 26.

that earliest Scandinavian kingship seems to have been associated with his cult rather than with Woden's.[48] However, Woden was more attractive to war-bands setting out from home and intent on vendetta, loot, or new lands to settle. They were often bound together in brotherhoods that achieved their greatest feats in a mood of ecstasy. All this made Woden an appropriate god. Can we go a step further and argue that evidence of the presence of Woden-worship is also evidence of the presence of a war-band divorced from its *gens* and free from the normal incubus of the kindred? Is a king who worships Woden no more than leader of a war-confederacy? If our answer is yes, then we shall have difficulty in explaining why other gods also accompanied the Germans to their final settlement-areas, and why Woden in his Roman guise was Mercury, the god of wealth and trade. No doubt trade was one aspect of any warrior-band's total life, but hardly the dominant one. I can more easily suppose that Woden's appeal was not exclusively to the warrior. The fact is, that, perhaps dazzled by Heroic literature, which naturally found its most rewarding theme in the loyalties of the war-band, we distinguish too sharply between warrior-bands and tribes. Both were involved in the German advances at all stages: the king who led his *comitatus* had other responsibilities—to kindreds, to tribes, and to peoples, however fragmentary. The cult of Woden will sometimes signify war-leadership, and the later we look the likelier it becomes. In the case of the Lombards we have an example. But Woden was not the only god, nor only the god of war, and certainly his cult is no proof that the kindred had been left behind or was fading away. It cannot be chance that of all the words that the Germans used to describe leadership, the one with the most distinctive future was *kuning* in its various forms— the head or representative of the kindred, tribe, or stock, or even quite simply '*the* kin'.[49] No argument based on semantic

[48] I am uncertain whether we should associate the subsequent royal Scandinavian cult of Odin primarily with successful prosecution of warlike activities. The evidence seems to conflict. See, for example, K. Hauck, 'Vom Kaiser- zum Götter-Amulett: die Bildformeln der Inschriften-Brakteaten', *Frühmittelalterliche Studien*, iii (1969), pp. 27–46; and K. Hald, 'The cult of Odin in Danish place-names', *Early English and Norse Studies*, ed. A. Brown and P. Foote (1963), pp. 99–109.

[49] Green, *The Carolingian Lord*, a book to which far too little attention has

considerations—as for instance the preponderance of Germanic *comitatus*, words in other contexts—can change the fact that the Germanic settlement of Roman Europe was a matter of hundreds of thousands of peasant cultivators and their families, not of enflamed *berserkir*. Kindreds and tribes are not disposed of by claiming that they were disintegrating. Chadwick himself, who held curious views about the disintegration of royal kindreds under stress of feud, still allowed that kindreds in general may well have retained much vitality.[50] If they did not, the barbarian laws are meaningless. Of the kindred and the king's relationship to it I shall wish to say more later. At this stage it is enough to insist that Woden and war-bands will not take us all the way to a sociology of the Germanic peoples.

A further point can be made about sacral kingship. If leadership of a war-band was not, at least essentially, a sacral role, it could become sacral, and quite quickly. The war-band leader was no doubt 'chosen' by his armed followers, in the sense that they would never follow a man they mistrusted; but the popular assembly, the *Thing*, might also be involved in the choice. That assembly was without question sacral in character. Those it selected for whatever task therefore had sacral authority behind them and in them.[51] How could the various strands in leadership possibly remain distinct? The ruler of a people was at one and the same time their link with the gods and their commander in battle. He would feel most at home with his kindred and people. Every German felt this.[52] He had the sense of being himself within a kin-structure; for his kin embraced the living and the dead; outside it was no honour, no luck, no peace, no life. Morally, the *comitatus* is an extension of the idea of loyalty implicit in kin-structure, and we need not regard it in any other

been paid by historians, discusses a semantic group of such words and reaches interesting conclusions; but he does not explain the victory of *kuning*, and I cannot follow him (p. 247) in seeing much in the argument of H. D. Kahl (*Zeitsch. der Sav. Stift., Germ. Abt.* lxxvii, pp. 154 ff.) that the word owes most to Frankish influence. He rightly stresses (p. 268) that Woden cannot always be taken for the divine leader of war-bands.

[50] *Heroic Age*, pp. 360–1.

[51] A point developed by O. Höfler, *Sakralcharakter*, p. 97, and J. de Vries, *Altgermanische Religionsgeschichte* (2nd ed., Berlin, 1956), p. 393.

[52] de Vries, *Religionsgeschichte*, p. 199, and *Die geistige Welt der Germanen* (Halle, 1945), p. 40.

light.[53] *Gens* and kin and war-band blend into one another to form a society. Kings have to do with every part of it. A case in point is that of the early Burgundians. Ammianus writes that 'among them a king (*rex*) has the general name of *Hendinos*, and according to ancient practice lays down his power and is deposed if under him the fortune of war has wavered or the crops have failed; just as the Egyptians commonly blame their rulers for such happenings. On the other hand, the Burgundians' priest, called a *Sinistus*, holds his power for life and is exposed to no such dangers as threaten kings.'[54] Some would like to interpret the *Sinistus* as a remnant of sacral kingship from a tribal past and the *Hendinos* as an up-to-date war-leader.[55] In other words, the Burgundians had two sorts of king at the same time. But Ammianus is clear that only the *Hendinos* is a king. Moreover, he is at once war-leader and something more, since he can be deposed for military failure or crop failure. We are not to suppose that either happened at all frequently, or the Burgundians would not have been the formidable people they were. As for the *Sinistus*, he is not superior to the king because he cannot be deposed; a priest, he simply enjoys security of tenure. Clearly the Burgundian king is no priest, but he is none the less the link between the gods and his people and must be a propitiation in times of ill-luck. It would be hard indeed to say that such a man was a straightforward *comitatus*-leader with no sacral background. The two cannot in practice be separated.

Let me summarize what I have so far said. The Tacitean *dux* is not the tap-root but a specialized function of Germanic kingship. Nothing suggests that the *rex* could not be a *dux* or that a *dux* could not acquire the traditional duties of a *rex*, or even that one was a much older office than the other. *Duces* rise and fall according to need, and so do *reges*. *Duces* who led confederations of warriors to victory and to new homes were either already of royal descent or soon found it desirable to claim that they

[53] W. Schlesinger, 'Herrschaft und Gefolgschaft in der germanisch-deutschen Verfassungsgeschichte', *Historische Zeitschrift*, clxxvii (1953), pp. 225–75, connects the *comitatus* with the peasantry.

[54] *Rer. Gest.* xxviii. v. 14.

[55] So Wenskus, *Stammesbildung*, excursus, who claims this as a possible exception to Schlesinger's dictum ('Heerkönigtum', p. 137) that a one-king people never had a *dux* or war-leader of the Tacitean type.

were. The reason for this is that one cannot for long separate the war-band from the kindred or either from the *gens*. However much the young warrior may crave new battles and more time in the mead-hall, his king has other duties; the functions of peace will tend to obtrude. There are crops to be raised, beasts to be reared, families to be settled, whether on new land or on old; and for all this, under divine protection, the king has responsibility.

The picture would be incomplete without some thought about the kingship of the greatest of the West Germanic peoples, the Franks.[56] As they first appear in Roman literature, they are not a homogeneous people but a confederation of tribes, to whom the name 'Franci' had been applied by themselves and by the Romans as a term of convenience without ethnical significance. Within their confederation were many tribes, each, it seems, headed by its own king with his own war-band, and still identified as such by the Romans in the fourth century. They had settled in the general area of the Lower and Middle Rhine, where the Romans used them as mercenaries. Many a Roman commander, and even some consuls, were chosen from the Rhineland Franks from the fourth century onwards. One may instance Silvanus, half-Frank, half-Roman, and a Christian, who went home to his German people in the end, taking with him who knows what ideas about Roman rule; and Mallobaudes, 'comes domesticorum et rex Francorum', who also went home.[57] Some Franks, but not all, may have been descendants of the Istaevones, as Tacitus claimed. One group—not a large one—was known as the Salians. They were the Franks of Toxandria, round the mouths of the Rhine. Some of them were exiled by Probus to the shores of the Black Sea, and the memory of this did not entirely fade. The evidence for their association with the sea is quite impressive. Their neighbours on the Rhine, the Sicambri, had a fleet, if Claudian is right.[58] John Lydus believed that 'Sicambri' was a general name for all Franks.[59] In later times, when northern Gaul had been occupied, the Franks seemed to be happy with

[56] For what follows see my *Long-Haired Kings*, ch. 7 (1), though I should now be prepared to give more weight to 'sacral' background than I did in 1962.
[57] Cf. Stroheker, *Germanentum und Spätantike*, ch. 1.
[58] *De Bello Gildonico*, line 373.
[59] *De Magistratibus*, i. 50.

a blend of Salian and Sicambric custom: there was no hasty abandonment of tribal traditions in the face of victorious war-leadership. Further east lay other Frankish tribes, notably the Ripuarians in the neighbourhood of Cologne. Two Frankish historians—Gregory of Tours in the sixth century and Fredegar in the seventh—were curious about the origins of Frankish kingship and looked back to the days before the advance into Gaul, to see what they could find. Gregory was worried by his chief source, Sulpicius Alexander, who appeared to discuss early Frankish chieftains in terms appropriate to kings without actually calling them so. Once his Franks were over the Rhine, however, in the *pagi* and *civitates*, it seemed certain to Gregory that they were ruled by kings. These were *reges criniti*, long-haired kings, which, if Civilis is any precedent, may hint at promotion through war-leadership; but they were also chosen for their *nobilitas*,[60] and this argues a different background. Descent counted for something, and they were meant to do more than fight. And this was natural, since their tribes were already settled on Roman agricultural land. In negotiating tribute or terms of peace or conditions of service, these kings would deal on behalf of their followers with the Romans, in whose interest it must have been to group tribes into larger formations of auxiliaries under a leadership they could understand and trust. Gregory of Tours, looking at the long-haired Merovingians of his own day, may have felt that there must have been something magic about the long hair of their predecessors. Originally it may have been no more than a sign that an oath had been taken, to lead a war-band in a particular engagement and this degenerated, later, into an old-fashioned hair-style denoting rank. What the Romans wanted was clear enough: a working arrangement with kings who could control their peoples, stabilize the troubled north, and protect rather than threaten Roman landlords; and for this money was available. They were not meant to be quietly absorbed by the Christian, Latin-speaking populations among whom they settled; nor were they. The sudden movement south of the Salians into northern Gaul, and of the Ripuarians west towards the Channel, brought some of their kings into greater

---

[60] *Lib. Hist.* ii. 9. Cf. Suetonius, *Galba*, ch. 2: 'quo paternam originem ad Iovem, maternam ad Pasiphaam Minonis uxorem referret.'

prominence. One particularly successful Salian king was
Childeric, who proved useful to the last Roman rulers of northern
Gaul and may even have paid a visit to Constantinople. He was
buried in Tournai. Part of his oft-pilfered burial treasure
survives. It is a various haul, rich in unique objects which we
cannot interpret and therefore call symbolic. There was splendid
war-gear, a cloak embroidered with some 300 gold 'cicadas', brace-
let and buckles, a miniature bull's-head in gold, the severed
head of a war-horse caparisoned in precious materials, a ring
bearing Childeric's name and a collection of gold and silver
coins. This was no leader of a small war-band but an established
federate king, well-to-do and in touch with a wider world than
the kingdom of Tournai. We cannot tell what gods Childeric
worshipped, but plainly they had done him proud. It was an
inheritance which his son Clovis would turn to good account.
Boldness in battle, joined to cunning, duplicity, ruthlessness,
and a well-timed conversion to Catholicism (all much admired
by Gregory) brought Clovis to overlordship in the Frankish
world and rule in Roman Gaul. If later genealogies may be
trusted, he would have taken his dynastic background seriously,
for he was a Merovingian, descended from the hero Merovech,
whose existence there is no ground for questioning. Fredegar,
interpolating Gregory, has a story about Merovech's birth.[61] He
records that Merovech's parents were taking a summer bathe in
the sea when the lady encountered a sea-beast—something like
Neptune or the Minotaur, he suggested. She forthwith conceived
Merovech. The dynasty thus saw its origins in a sea-beast that
was part-bull, part-man.[62] One is put in mind of the bull's head
in Childeric's treasure and the sea connections of the Salian
Franks. These could have meant little to Fredegar and his contemporaries; so little that one is tempted to see the beginnings
of the legend in a time much nearer the migration period. So far
as we know, the Merovingians never claimed to be descended
from Woden or any other god;[63] but their beginnings were not
seen as ordinary and were not overlooked when the dynasty

[61] *Hist.* iii. 9.

[62] See K. Hauck, *Saeculum*, vi (1955), pp. 186–223.

[63] Schlesinger, 'Heerkönigtum', p. 139, thinks that the Merovingians must
have worshipped Woden in order to achieve a sacral character. But this they
may have had already.

made fresh headway as Catholic converts, dear to the Roman Church and approved by the emperors in Constantinople.[64] Through all of Clovis's reign there runs the dual strand familiar in that of Theodoric: the great Germanic warlord surrounded by his *trustis* (or armed following), and the barbarian anxious to profit from whatever skills he could pick up from the Romans. His *Lex Salica*, to which I shall return, is inconceivable without the help of professionals trained in Roman Vulgar Law; yet its content is Germanic. He made the best of both worlds and improved on Theodoric by getting away with it, doubtless because he was no Arian but a Catholic. Yet the enduring roots of his kingship lay in something old and tribal, and they were not at all affected by the subjection to his rule of neighbouring Frankish tribes with no Merovingian tradition, as well as of Germanic tribes still further afield, like the Alamans and the Thuringians. Merovingian subjection of another people called for a shield-raising to mark a break in the normal succession, but no more.[65] Multiple rule will obviously add to a king's fame and increase his capacity to reward the faithful with loot and land, but it will no more alter the nature of his kingship than will the opportunity to tax Roman citizens. The tenacity with which the Merovingians held on to their sacral background does something to explain their survival through two and a half centuries of declining military power. They were what the Franks expected them to be: successful in an archaic way. Whatever the Church might say, they could persist in the ancient Germanic practice of polygamy; and physical contact with them could heal the sick, as Gregory explains in a well-known tale about King Guntramn.[66] If we had a Frankish equivalent of *Beowulf*, who can doubt that it would portray a Merovingian in his hall, lavishing gifts on faithful warriors, and fighting lustily against odds? And it would mislead

[64] I agree with K. Hauck, 'Von einer spätantiken Randkultur zum karolingischen Europa', *Frühmittelalterliche Studien*, i (1967), pp. 24 ff., 30 ff., 43 ff., when he associates Clovis's recognition at Tours, baptism, and assumption of a *cathedra regni* in Paris as aspects of his entry into the orbit of the Empire.
[65] Trans-Rhenan Germans subjected to the Franks seem to have regarded their new rulers, native or Frankish, as *reges*, though to the Merovingians they were only *duces*. The English always considered that the Frisians were ruled by *reges*, and the Lombards that the Bavarians were so ruled, though both Frisian and Bavarian rulers are called *duces* in Frankish sources.
[66] *Lib. Hist.* ix. 21.

us into believing that this was all Germanic kingship was about. The early Merovingians were great warriors, which is more than can be said of the many royal dynasties they overthrew; but this made them successful; kings, it did not make them. The Roman Church made them *reges christiani,* but this, too, had little immediate effect on their view of themselves. Descendants of a sea-beast, they held the loyalty of the Frankish peasant-cultivator, brought a blessing on his crops and fruitfulness to his family, warded off disease, and feuded among themselves without the loss of any mystique that mattered. Beyond this, as with other barbaric dynasties, settlement in a Roman province revealed weakness, an uncertainty about what an old-fashioned dynasty in a fresh political context could do. The Romans got part of what they wanted: massive settlements of Germanic soldiers ruled by kings who had *potestas*. They could arrange treaties, hand out the presents, and fight as required. That is the aspect of kingly activity that Roman writers were interested in. Such kings were teachable; if they were not yet *filii* of a paternalistic emperor, they were in a fair way to becoming so. And the Church, in so far as it interested itself in the fourth- and fifth-century barbarians, could proffer them a god who was just as willing as Woden to accept military service. What exactly was in this for the Germanic tribes themselves remained an open question.

One Merovingian princess, great-granddaughter of Clovis and a Catholic from Paris, was sent abroad to marry into a Germanic family that was not only pagan but intended to stay that way; a family that claimed descent from Hengest and Horsa.

II

KING ÆTHELBERHT

WHETHER we regard the English invaders and settlers of Roman Britain as close-knit tribes or as the 'convenient stream of flotsam' dismissed by Jolliffe,[1] their leaders remain equally obscure. Chadwick[2] found it 'scarcely credible' that they could have been more than '*principes*', by which he probably understood mercenary captains competent to manage the Germanic 'flotsam' as it drifted from the continent westward. Kemble, on the other hand, who devoted some valuable pages to Anglo-Saxon kingship, preferred to think of them as not primarily war-leaders at all, but as peace-keepers or judges of their tribes. 'I believe', he wrote, that 'the original king was a judge, who super-induced the warlike upon his peaceful functions.'[3] However, this did not prevent Kemble from seeing the earliest English kingdoms as 'camps . . . not seldom in a state of mutual hostility'.[4] In fact, one can suppose that kingship of every type was represented among these early leaders. There will have been big men and little, *duces ex virtute* but also *reges ex nobilitate,* and sometimes both combined in the same persons. We ought not to be too ready to scrap the old theory of fairly large tribal units in our anxiety to make room for the riff-raff of settlers who here and there betray themselves in place-names. The British, who were not helpless or unable to offer resistance, were, in the end, overcome—presumably by considerable forces whose commanders knew what they were doing. Vortigern, like other resistance leaders of the Empire, bit off more than he could chew. It seems pointless to speculate how many of the successful English leaders would have started as *reges ex nobilitate,* or have represented themselves as such once they had secured a foothold. Nor can we

---

[1] *Pre-Feudal England: the Jutes* (1933), p. 117.
[2] *Heroic Age*, p. 376.
[3] *The Saxons in England*, ii, p. 41.
[4] Ibid., p. 23.

know if Romano-British example led to any early modification of their ideas of rule. One can see a shadowy Gwledig behind the first Bretwalda[5] (who ruled over an area notably un-British), but there is no cogent reason why one should. It is significant, I think, that a great British prince of a later time, Hywel Dha, had to look to the Anglo-Saxons for a model of high-kingship. He had inherited none.[6]

Take the case of Kent—the Romano-British *civitas Cantiacorum*. Nothing that we know of its first English rulers would warrant the conclusion that they were indebted to those they replaced, as lords of the region, even though they may have accepted something of its administrative shape and, if place-name evidence means anything, certainly did not expel all the *Cantiaci* they found there.[7] Their earliest grave-goods betray at least some willingness to profit from established arts and crafts. Their first rulers, according to tradition, were Hengest and Horsa.[8] Neither their duality nor their curious names compel us to dismiss them as fiction; dual, and even triple, rule was not unknown to the continental Germans, and there were certainly names as implausible as theirs. Moreover, there was a continental Hengest, of the Danish tribe of the *Eota* according to *Beowulf* and the Finn Fragment, who may very well have been identical with the Kentish king.[9] Nevertheless, later Kentish kings saw themselves as descendants of Oisc, calling themselves *Oiscingas*. Oisc as a personal name is recorded only by Bede; but the fact that it seemed plausible to him, and those who informed him and read him, is not without importance. Sir Frank Stenton concluded that 'the historic Hengest is best regarded as a chief of very noble descent who brings his own retinue from over sea to

[5] As does Margaret Deanesly, 'Roman traditionalist influence among the Anglo-Saxons', *English Historical Review*, lviii (1943). C. E. Stevens, however, contends that *Gwledig* does not mean lord of a country but commander of a local militia (*Études celtiques*, 1938, p. 90).

[6] So D. A. Binchy argues, *Celtic and Anglo-Saxon Kingship*, p. 22.

[7] See Kenneth Jackson, *Language and History in Early Britain* (1953), p. 246.

[8] Bede, *Hist. Eccl.* i. 15. I have used Plummer's edition throughout, that of Colgrave and Mynors having appeared too late.

[9] Cf. Chadwick, *Heroic Age*, pp. 49–50. Dr. J. N. L. Myres, *Anglo-Saxon Pottery and the Settlement of England* (1969), p. 96, n. 2, sees no reason to doubt the identification of the two Hengests. It has, however, been questioned by Ferdinand Lot, *Recueil des travaux historiques*, i (1968), p. 746, and by Mrs. Turville-Petre, 'Hengest and Horsa', especially p. 289.

Britain . . . and fights various battles which open the way to an occupation of Kent by men of his race in the next generation.[10] The tradition that Oisc was Hengest's son is not disproved thereby. But the point is this: whether we see Hengest and Horsa and Oisc as mythical figures from a common Germanic stock of divine founders or as shadows of historical reality,[11] they survived the overthrow of Kentish paganism to become the royal past of Æthelberht's house. They were not mythical to Bede, nor, I suppose, to the critical churchmen in Canterbury with whom he was in touch. Christian kings needed pagan ancestors of heroic standing.

Another tradition reported by Bede was that these first Kentish kings ruled not Angles or Saxons or Frisians or Franks, but Jutes. He seemed quite sure of this: it was a simple fact. I am prepared to accept it, even if I am uncertain what he means; but not without first inquiring (since it matters in my present context) if there is a serious case for regarding Bede's Jutes as Franks. What is the case? First, the archaeology of Jutish Kent bears strong traces of Frankish cultural influence, notably in the grave-goods of women; secondly, Kent shows some institutional and social traits that may have parallels in the area of the Middle Rhine; and thirdly, it is inherently likely that the Franks, while setting up house in Gaul, should have thrown off a fragmentary settlement in Kent. How good is the case? As to grave-goods— and here I speak as a child—the more firmly we hold that Kent was in continuous contact with the continent, the likelier it surely becomes that the grave-goods of Frankish provenance were largely the result of trade: their quantity, after all, was not unlimited. This is not to say that some Franks did not accompany the early settlers, or come later. The most recent attempt[12] to people southern England with Franks has been dismissed by Dr. Myres, after careful examination, as unproven.[13] The Rhineland

[10] *Anglo-Saxon England* (1943), p. 17.

[11] The work of de Vries, Dumézil, and others on the common Germanic background of gods and kings points the way to a new field of study, but to my mind is still too conjectural to be used with confidence in the specific field of early English kingship.

[12] Vera Evison, *The Fifth-Century Invasions South of the Thames* (1965).

[13] *English Historical Review*, lxxxi (1966), p. 345. There is still much to be learnt from Dr. Myres's review of Jolliffe in *Archaeological Journal*, xc (1933), pp. 156–60.

parallels, so compellingly drawn by Jolliffe,[14] strike me as in-
conclusive at best. They depend too much upon similarities in
Kentish and Ripuarian law to command ready assent. Like
Chadwick,[15] I cannot help noting the dissimilarities between the
Frankish social system and those of other Germanic peoples,
Jutes included, and in particular I should place little reliance on
any comparison of wergeld values here and abroad. Professor
Hawkes, attracted by Jolliffe's thesis, as we all are, yet wary of
the Middle Rhine,[16] postulates a late Frankish settlement of
Kent from the general area of the Lower Rhine and will not tie
down his Franks more closely than to call them, in the manner
of Tacitus, *Istaevones*—that is, one of the classical divisions of
the Germanic peoples, distinct from the *Ingaevones* to whom the
Angles and Saxons belonged. It may indeed be true that more
Franks settled in Kent in the sixth century than earlier. But
Franks were Franks, and by them we must surely mean Germans
who spoke a tongue that was not that from which early Kentish
developed, even if Frankish were intelligible to speakers of early
Kentish. If the language of the main settlers of Kent ever belonged to the same group as Frankish, we are faced with the
task of explaining how later Kentish had lost all trace of its
origins.[17]

One could possibly find some support for the view that many
Jutes were Franks from the connection of the Kentish royal
house with the Merovingians. But this goes back no further
than the marriage of Æthelberht to Bertha, daughter of King
Charibert of Paris, perhaps in the 560s. Why did it take place?
Stenton connects it with the conquest, at about the same time, by
Charibert's brother, King Chilperic, of the Euthiones, who lived
somewhere on the northern fringe of Francia. The Euthiones
would have been Jutes and, for Stenton, 'clearly represent the
remnant of this nation which had not taken part in the migration

---

[14] *Pre-Feudal England*, esp. pp. 39, 59, 111–15.

[15] *Heroic Age*, p. 351.

[16] 'The Jutes of Kent', *Dark-Age Britain* (1956); note also the warning of
H. Arbman in *Medieval Archaeology*, i (1957), p. 173, and Leeds's rejoinder in
the same volume.

[17] See A. Campbell, *Old English Grammar* (1959), p. 4. I am grateful to Professor Campbell for further reassurance on this point.

to Kent.[18] Hunter Blair, however, fastens upon a movement in the other direction, for which Procopius is the evidence. Procopius, writing in the mid sixth century, understood that the English, the Frisians, and the British sent annual contingents to Francia, where they settled, 'and by these means [the Franks] say that they are winning over the island'.[19] Further evidence for this Frankish claim is a letter, dated July 596,[20] from Gregory the Great to the Frankish kings Theuderic and Theudebert, commending St. Augustine to their care. He begins by praising their Christian rectitude and goes on: 'I have every reason to think that you heartily wish your subjects [*subiectos vestros*] to be converted to the same faith as yourselves, their kings and lords— Atque ideo pervenit ad nos Anglorum gentem ad fidem Christianum . . . velle converti.' The only escape from *subiectos vestros* is to suppose that Gregory did not mean what he said, or was ill-informed, but he was quite well-informed about Frankish affairs as a whole. The dependence, whatever it meant, was there in his eyes. I think Stenton was right to argue that marriage into the great Merovingian house would have implied some sort of political dependence for the Kentish kings; and it is precisely as far back as that marriage that one can trace the dependence, such as it was. If we need to explain the marriage on grounds other than mere propinquity, we may see its cause in the situation envisaged by Procopius: namely, that many English (Jutes included) migrated to Francia. But none of this will make the Kentish Jutes Franks. Gregory, for his part, was clear that the people who needed conversion were Angles, not Franks. What proportion of the Kentish Jutes came from the continental home of the Euthiones, and what from Jutland direct, and how many returned to the continent, we shall never know.[21] But we may well ponder the words of Dr. Myres, apropos early Kentish pottery: 'It is significant, in view of the literary traditions of Jutish settlement in Kent, that the closest parallels of all come from Jutland

---

[18] *Anglo-Saxon England*, p. 59.

[19] *Hist.* viii. xx. 6–10; Peter Hunter Blair, *Roman Britain and Early England* (1963), p. 164.

[20] *Reg.* vi. 49.

[21] N. Wagner, *Getica* (Berlin, 1967), pp. 60 ff., rightly discounts the theory that Jordanes, *Getica*, 38 is evidence that the Jutes were connected with the Goths.

itself, where pottery of very similar forms and decoration has
been recorded from at least twelve places, mostly in western
coastal areas . . . , then as now the natural point of departure for
a voyage both to Frisia and to south-eastern Britain.'[22] We know
that the Merovingians had a large array of *subiecti* who were not
Franks. Why should they not have included our Jutes?

Whatever the relationship between the Merovingians and the
Kentish kings, there is no evidence that the marriage turned the
Kentish court into something that it was not before. Professor
Deanesly writes that 'it seems likely . . . that Æthelberht had
a court and officers on the Frankish plan, and that the introduction of writing to Kent came with the copying of Frankish
methods of government before the coming of Augustine'.[23] No
doubt Bertha corresponded with her relatives (Gregory says she
was learned in letters), and Bishop Liudhard, too, with former
colleagues; and there is a good case for believing that Kentish
charters may have been in existence from Augustine's time,
though not before.[24] But none of this will turn Canterbury into
a Merovingian court. Æthelberht inherited no secular officials
trained in the continental schools. He was no Merovingian. He
did not even mint his own coins. This may have been because
he was unable to command moneyers sufficiently skilled, though
the medal, issue to which Liudhard's surviving 'coin' belongs,
would seem to discredit that.[25] Clearly his people had use for a
coinage, and presumably he would have known that coins could
be struck in the names of kings: the Frank Theudebert issued
coinage bearing his name in quite large quantities. Perhaps
Æthelberht hesitated to ape his superiors' practice and preferred to use coins that reached Kent in the ordinary course of
trade.

[22] *Anglo-Saxon Pottery*, p. 95.

[23] 'Early English and Gallic Minsters', *Trans. R. Hist. Soc.* 4th series, xxiii,
p. 62.

[24] I am persuaded by Dr. P. Chaplais, 'The origin and authenticity of the
royal Anglo-Saxon diploma', *Journal of the Society of Archivists*, iii. 2 (1965),
p. 51, that we ought to take seriously the view of Kemble that written diplomas
were in use in Augustine's Kent. See further Chaplais's 'Who introduced
charters into England? The case for Augustine', ibid. iii. 10. (1969).

[25] See P. Grierson, 'The Canterbury (St. Martin's) hoard of Frankish and
Anglo-Saxon coin-ornaments', *British Numismatic Journal*, xxvii (1953),
pp. 41–3.

The most significant respect in which he did not ape the Merovingians was in religion. Bertha, with Liudhard her chaplain, did not convert her husband to Christianity. He remained a pagan, almost to the end of his life. There is cause for surprise here; not surprise that the Franks let things slide: they had no experience yet of the missionary work that was soon to develop in conjunction with colonizing activity in the Rhineland, and Frankish bishops would hardly interest themselves in the English who lived, after all, in a former Roman province where the British were still actively Christian. When Gregory of Tours interviewed Queen Bertha's mother, she seems to have had nothing to tell him about the *Ganthia* to which her daugher had gone as a bride. The surprise is that Bertha herself should have done nothing. The religious traditions of her family were far from passive. When her cousin, Ingundis, married the Visigoth Hermenigild in about the year 570,[26] she not merely refused to be converted to Arianism but helped to convert her husband to Catholicism. Their great-grandmother, Chrotechildis, had had much to do with the conversion from paganism of Clovis himself.[27] Queen Theudelinda, a Bavarian, almost won over her Lombard husband to Catholicism.[28] Paganism in Kent was different because it was successful. How deeply rooted and widespread it was, was shown by Stenton in a remarkable paper.[29] Place-names betray the worship of Thor and Woden among the Jutes, though of course not necessarily so late as Æthelberht. However, 'five undoubted places of heathen worship can still be identified within a radius of twelve miles from Augustine's church of Canterbury'.[30] Woodnesborough, in north Kent, could show, until comparatively recently, the *beorg* of Woden, from which it took its name; nearby, at Coombe, lay the cremated remains of a sixth-century warrior who, as like as not, worshipped at the *beorg*; and at Finglesham, also near, has been found a seventh-century buckle showing a warrior with spears who strongly suggests the cult of Woden, a cult as characteristic of

[26] Gregory of Tours, *Lib. Hist.* iv. 38.   [27] Ibid. ii. 28–30.
[28] Almost, but not quite. Cf. Gregory I's letter of December 603 to Theudelinda (*Reg.* xiv. 12). Paul the Deacon, *Hist. Lang.* iv. 6, goes too far.
[29] 'The historical bearing of place-name studies: Anglo-Saxon heathenism', *Trans. R. Hist. Soc.* 4th series, xxiii (1941), pp. 1–24.
[30] Ibid., p. 23.

the Jutes as it is uncharacteristic of the Franks.[31] Though King
Eorconberht ordered the destruction of idols,[32] there is no evidence that his predecessor Æthelberht did. Why should he have
done? It may have been under his pagan gods that he won
military overlordship throughout central and southern England,
and held it, at least till the rise of Redwald in East Anglia. His
ultimate conversion, by missionaries who were neither Frankish
nor British but Roman, may perhaps betray some waning of his
star, though not his abandonment of all that he understood by
paganism. In general, Germanic conversions of this period signi-
fied not total abandonment of the pagan gods but acceptance of
an additional god.[33] The good catholic King Theudebert, according to Procopius, sacrificed Ostrogothic women and children as
the first-fruits of victory when he won control over a bridge at
Pavia: 'These barbarians, though they have become Christians,'
remarked the historian, 'preserve the greater part of their ancient
religion; for they still make human sacrifices of an unholy
nature, and it is in connection with these that they make their
prophesies.'[34] Lex Salica, promulgated by the Christian Clovis,
records the punishment for theft of sacrificial pigs.[35] Æthelberht
could scarcely be expected to do better; nor did he. What sets one
wondering, however, is not the possible effect of conversion on
Æthelberht and his followers,[36] but why he consented to be

[31] See H. R. Ellis Davidson, 'The Smith and the Goddess', Frühmittelalterliche
Studien, iii (1969), pp. 225–6, and Sonia Hawkes et al, 'The Finglesham Man',
Antiquity, xxxix (1965). How are we to interpret the martial figure of Christ
on the funerary plaque from Grésin (Puy-de-Dôme)? (E. Salin, La Civilisation
mérovingienne, iv (1959), pl. xi, facing p. 400). He holds a spear in a manner
highly suggestive of the Finglesham Man. If this hints at the residue of a
Woden-cult among a group of Franks in the seventh century, it would not be
surprising, or affect the view that it was uncharacteristic of the Franks as a
whole. It raises interesting questions. I am obliged to Mr. James Campbell for
reminding me of the plaque.   [32] Bede, Hist. Eccl. iii. 8.

[33] It is a type of conversion classified as adhesion by A. D. Nock, Conversion (1933), p. 16.

[34] Hist. vi. xxv. 7–10. See also Averil Cameron, 'Agathias on the early
Merovingians', Annali della Scuola Normale Superiore di Pisa, 2nd series,
xxxvii (1968), appendix D, 'The composition of Theudebert's army in 539'.

[35] Lex Salica (65-title text), ii. 16. For comment from the archaeological side,
see E. Salin, La Civilisation mérovingienne, iv (Paris, 1959), p. 43.

[36] The 10,000 English conversions to which Pope Gregory refers in a letter
to Eulogius of Alexandria (Reg. viii. 29) are perhaps more likely to represent
the pope's idea of Æthelberht's armed following than the ordinary run of
peasants. Correctio rusticorum was surely another matter.

converted at all. He had neither sought nor obtained conversion at Merovingian hands; political strings could have been attached, as they had been in the case of the Burgundians, whose movement away from Arianism towards Catholicism had facilitated the work of Frankish conquest; and it may not have been offered him. But by 596 or earlier he was ready to consider it from Rome, as Pope Gregory was aware. The course of that conversion is well enough known, and is not, in my opinion, affected by arguments recently advanced by Dom Brechter,[37] and by Mr. Richardson and Professor Sayles.[38] I merely note that, from Rome's viewpoint, it was a major undertaking. We are too apt to see Augustine as a nobody and his companions as a tremulous handful. The mission was forty-strong, plus interpreters. No one but Pope Gregory could have fielded such a team. It included some very able men; the material traces of their work are not lightly to be dismissed.[39] Augustine himself, chosen head of Gregory's private monastery in Rome, had special qualifications for missionary work as Gregory understood it. Notably, he was a biblical scholar.[40] Of the books he would have brought with him to Canterbury—psalters, missals, commentaries, and the like—the one that survives as probably his is a gospel-book (Corpus Christi College, Cambridge, MS. 286). This qualification of Augustine's was special, because the heart of Gregorian conversion lay in the Bible and the application of its message to Germanic kings. Æthelberht himself left no clue to what he thought Christianity

---

[37] Suso Brechter, *Die Quellen zur Angelsachsenmission Gregors des Grossen* (Münster, 1941), and 'Die Bekehrung der Angelsachsen', *Settimane di Studio del Centro Italiano di Studi sull'Alto Medioevo*, xiv (Spoleto, 1967), pp. 191–215. See the criticisms of R. A. Markus, 'The chronology of the Gregorian mission to England', *Journ. Eccl. Hist.* xiv. 1, pp. 16–30, and of Paul Meyvaert, 'Bede and Gregory the Great', *Jarrow Lecture*, 1964.
[38] *Law and Legislation from Æthelberht to Magna Carta* (1966), ch. i and appendix i. The authors do, however, raise some legitimate doubts on other aspects of Kentish history.
[39] These are summarized by R. L. S. Bruce-Mitford, 'The reception by the Anglo-Saxons of Mediterranean art, following their conversion from Ireland and Rome', *Settimane di Studio*, xiv, pp. 798–825. For Augustine's school, see Bede, *Hist. Eccl.* iii. 18.
[40] Ibid. i. 32, and Gregory, *Reg.* xi. 37. See also R. Kottje, *Studien zum Einfluss des Alten Testaments auf Recht und Liturgie des frühen Mittelalters (VI.–VIII. Jahrh.)* (Bonn, 1964) for one way in which the Bible could affect kings.

had done for him; but by analogy we can form some idea. There survives a letter, written, at about the time of Æthelberht's death, by the Visigoth king Sisebut to his Lombard colleague Adaloald, urging his conversion from Arianism to Catholicism.[41] Sisebut is quite clear about the material advantages of Catholicism: in the old days, he says, the Goths suffered from every sort of misfortune—constant wars, harvest failures, plague, and so on—but now all that has changed, for within the Catholic peace 'Gotorum viget imperium'. One might call the tone a trifle cynical, and so, too, the appeal to self-interest when Sisebut goes on to draw the moral from the *locus classicus* for Petrine authority, St. Matthew 16:18–19. He gives us what amounts to a preview of King Oswiu at Whitby. Pope Gregory left Æthelberht in no doubt that these considerations also entered into his conception of the conversion of kings. He wrote to assure the new convert that a Christian king's gifts were special and came from God, who would render his fame more glorious to posterity.[42] In a word, something is being offered to take the place of the pagan basis, whatever it was, of the king's prestige. Gregory cites the example of the Emperor Constantine:[43] help Augustine, he urges, and Augustine will help you with God. In short, Æthelberht may count on his place in the kingdom of heaven, the literal sense of which, as a noble city ruled over by the king of kings, is never far from his mind. But the king may also count on stability for his present kingdom, on good fortune and prosperity and enduring fame for his dynasty. Other papal letters to English kings of the next generation were to labour the same point. This was not an occasion when the pope found it expedient to emphasize something else that was much in his thoughts and discussed at other times:[44] namely, that the true basis of all earthly rule was humility. Like Augustine of Hippo, he derived this from

[41] *MGH Epist. Mero.* i. pp. 671–5; also J. Fontaine, 'Conversion et culture chez les Wisigoths d'Espagne', *Settimane di Studio*, xiv, p. 134.

[42] Bede, *Hist. Eccl.* i. 32. Cf. my 'Gregory of Tours and Bede: their views on the personal qualities of kings', *Frühmittelalterliche Studien*, ii (1968), p. 39. Gregory's views on kingship are examined by H. H. Anton, *Fürstenspiegel und Herrscherethos in der Karolingerzeit* (Bonn, 1968), pp. 364–405.

[43] See the important study of Eugen Ewig, 'Das Bild Constantins der Gr. im frühen Mittelalter', *Hist. Jahrb.* lxxv (1956).

[44] e.g. *Moralia in Job*, Migne, *Pat. Lat.* lxxvi, esp. 203c and 377a–b. Cf. Augustine, *De Civ. Dei*, v. 24 and xix. 15.

his belief in the equality of all men. Any man placed above his fellows filled a God-given office, a *ministerium*, and Gregory is the first to call kingship an office. It thus followed that a king should never overlook the moral root of his power. Medieval preoccupation with kingly *humilitas* and *superbia* was mainly to rest upon Gregory's interpretation of Augustine, reinforced by the Bible: rule is a service, and the man who exercises it will fail when he forgets that he is a man. One sees why King Æthelberht might not have welcomed this part of the missionary message, at least to begin with. It was enough for him that conversion could be identified with victory and that the warfare proper to a Bretwalda had a Christian justification. What was Christian war and peace? Peace was God's peace and God's gift, won by fighting his enemies and compelling the observation of his commands. In this sense, war *was* peace. Such had been the warfare of the People of Israel, at once more mystical and more tremendous than any heroic feat by a Germanic warrior. Thus the Hebraic tradition came to reinforce the other traditions of warfare to which Æthelberht was heir: the Roman, namely, with its message that peace was born of victory, and the Germanic, where war was a manifestation of vitality.[45]

It seems to me that there were two possible (and conflicting) reasons why Æthelberht should have accepted conversion when he did. The first is that he had made himself a powerful king by force of arms. That he should then wish to enter the community of what might be called Gregorian kings would seem natural enough, once he had been persuaded of the advantages and reassured that the Merovingian grip upon his house would not be tightened thereby. The other reason is that by 596 he may already have passed the zenith of his power. The incident at Augustine's Oak was a reverse for Æthelberht as well as Augustine. Bede records that 'while Æthelberht was still living, [Redwald, the East Anglian king] had already obtained predominance for his people—qui etiam vivente Ædilbercto eidem suae genti ducatum praebebat, obtinuit'.[46] Kemble took this to mean that Redwald actually deprived Æthelberht of his ascendancy

---

[45] Cf. the interesting comments of Gina Fasoli, 'Pace e guerra nell'alto medioevo occidentale', *Settimane di Studio*, xv, i (Spoleto, 1968).
[46] *Hist. Eccl.* ii. 5.

over the southern English;[47] it is more likely to mean that Redwald's rise to power even in his own country was unwelcome to the overlord. But if Kemble is right, Æthelberht is likely to have suffered reverses in battle or at least to have had the humiliation of relinquishing whatever services a Bretwalda could extract from subordinate kings. We cannot tell if this happened before or after his conversion: the date of Redwald's succession is itself uncertain. Defeat, or the threat of it, and ill fortune of any kind, were common grounds for a pagan king to try his luck with Christianity before his people deprived him of his rule, or indeed for a Christian king, in England as on the continent, to think again about the advantages of paganism. But Kemble was guessing; and it is surely more likely that Æthelberht's conversion coincided with an increase in power than with a decrease.

When the pope reminded Æthelberht of the example of Constantine and Queen Bertha of that of Helena,[48] as he also reminded other kings and queens, he meant it to be understood that the new convert was entering the family of Catholic kings of whom the emperor was the father. Papal and imperial correspondence of the period leaves no doubt about this.[49] He assures Bertha that 'bona vestra' have been reported not merely in Rome but even in Constantinople, where they have reached the ears of the 'serenissimum principem'. Politically this might mean little or nothing. But one certain consequence would be that the new convert would enter into the tradition of written law of which the emperor was the fountain-head. This is one reason why Æthelberht's laws must be dated after his conversion. Lawbooks were a Roman, and specifically a Christian-Roman, gift to the Germanic kings.

We may start with Bede's words about law in Kent. They occur in a chapter isolated from his account of Augustine's mission but correctly placed in relation to the date of Æthelberht's death.[50] It was the right moment to summarize the great king's achievements. Bede notes, among other benefits that Æthelberht's

---

[47] *Saxons in England*, ii, p. 14.

[48] *Reg.* xi. 35.

[49] The matter is discussed by F. Dölger, 'Die Familie der Könige im Mittelalter', reprinted in his *Byzanz und die europäische Staatenwelt* (Darmstadt, 1964), pp. 34–69.

[50] *Hist. Eccl.* ii. 5.

people obtained, the writing down of 'decreta iudiciorum, iuxta exempla Romanorum'. What was more, these were written 'Anglorum sermone' and were still observed in Kent. The first law dealt with restitution for theft of church property. Bede goes on to provide a short Kentish king-list. There are several problems here, that are bound to affect our view of what sort of king Æthelberht was.

In the first place, what is to be understood by *exempla Romanorum?* Augustine could have brought some Roman law with him to Canterbury. 'It is of course quite possible', in Maitland's words, 'that a few of the more learned among the clergy may at times have studied some books of Roman law',[51] even in Augustine's Canterbury. Yet nothing of Roman law can be discerned in Æthelberht's *decreta*, beyond the bare fact that both were written. If we look further afield for the *Romani* whose *exempla* Æthelberht's mentors provided, we might see an implied reference to church law. Bede certainly used *Romani* to describe Roman clergy, as in the passage where he states that James the Deacon introduced Gregorian chant to York 'iuxta morem Romanorum'.[52] The usage was not unknown in Theodore's Canterbury.[53] Early penitential codes do indeed have certain features in common with barbarian law. But it is a long shot. An easier explanation is that the *exempla* were continental laws brought over by the Roman missionaries. But which laws? We need to place Æthelberht's laws where they belong, within the body of a legal tradition that goes back to the codex of the Visigoth king Euric, composed in southern Gaul between 466 and 484.[54] This codex survives in a fragmentary state,[55] and no one familiar with it could claim that it was a likely model for Kentish

---

[51] Pollock and Maitland, *History of English Law before the Time of Edward I* (1895), i, p. xxxii.

[52] *Hist. Eccl.* ii. 20.

[53] e.g. Eddius, *Vita Wilfridi*, ch. 43: 'in omni sapientia et in iudiciis Romanorum eruditissimum'; and Theodore's Penitential, v. 2: 'qui numquam Romanorum decreta mutari a se sepe jam dicebat voluisse' (Haddan and Stubbs, *Councils and Ecclesiastical Documents*, iii, p. 181).

[54] On the date and composition see R. Buchner, *Die Rechtsquellen* (Weimar, 1953), pp. 7–9 (Wattenbach-Levison, *Deutschlands Geschichtsquellen im Mittelalter*), and Stroheker, 'Die geschichtliche Stellung der ostgermanischen Staaten am Mittelmeer', *Germanentum und Spätantike*, pp. 122 ff.

[55] Ed. K. Zeumer, *MGH Legum* Sect. I, vol. i (1902).

law. But a century later another king, Liuvigild, legislated for the Goths. Three hundred and nineteen chapters of that legislation were preserved in a notable collection of law made in the mid-seventh century by King Reccaswinth, who designated them *antiqua*. When we look at these *antiqua* we come a lot nearer to Æthelberht. For example, Book III contains matter on women and marriage that can at least be compared with Æthelberht's section of regulations affecting women; Book V starts with a section *de ecclesiasticis rebus*; VI 4 (2) covers penalties for breaking in, robbery, and homicide; VII 2 (10) enacts that theft from the king shall be compensated ninefold; and VII 3 (3) clearly admits the kin's responsibility at law. Finally, a king-list is added to the manuscripts of Reccaswinth's law, which may already have been present, less the intervening kings, in Liuvigild's law. One again recalls that Bede, who seems to have seen a manuscript of Æthelberht's law, adds a Kentish king-list. Visigothic law, whether of Euric or Liuvigild or Reccaswinth, was quickly disseminated in western Europe. It lies, with much else, behind the earliest law-book of the Lombards of Italy, that of King Rothari. This huge *edictum* of 388 chapters contains some close parallels to Kentish law—so close, that some have argued from them a common background, either in blood or in original settlement-area, for the Lombards and the Kentings.[56] But we cannot claim that Æthelberht's *exemplum* was Lombardic, for Rothari's *edictum* is a little too late in date, and it contains the explicit statement that Rothari himself was the first to write down his people's laws.[57] Liuvigild's work was certainly available to Rothari: from it he borrowed a phrase, derived ultimately from Justinian's seventh *Novella*, to the effect that he had corrected the laws of his people, emended them, and added or subtracted material as he thought best. The same occurs in the preface to

[56] Cf. H. Brunner, *Deutsche Rechtsgeschichte* (3rd ed., Berlin, 1961), i, p. 537; Buchner, 'Die römischen und die germanischen Wesenszüge in der neuen politischen Ordnung des Abendlandes', *Settimane di Studio*, v. i (Spoleto, 1958), pp. 258, 262 ff.; Gian Piero Bognetti, 'L'editto di Rotari come espediente politico di una monarchia barbarica' and 'Frammenti di uno studio sulla composizione dell'editto di Rotari', both in *L'età longobarda*, iv. (Milan, 1968).

[57] Ed. F. Beyerle, *Die Gesetze der Langobarden* (Weimar, 1947), ch. 386, p. 156.

King Alfred's laws. But Rothari's skilled compilators also had at their disposal the texts of Frankish, Burgundian, and other Germanic laws and often fall back on them, thus drawing upon the whole available Germanic experience of law-writing in their determination to give their king a great legal document that might consolidate his royal authority over the peoples he ruled.[58] These texts included the written laws of his dynasty's predecessors in Italy, the Ostrogoths. Their historian, Jordanes, states that their laws were written, and observed *usque nunc*—in the mid-sixth century, that is.[59] These laws were called *Belagines* by the Goths. Whether they were in the vernacular or in Latin we cannot tell, since they no longer exist.[60] What we do know is that some of the Roman advisers of the last Ostrogoths found employment at the court of the first Lombard kings, and it is not to be supposed that they would have failed to draw their new masters' attention to the advantages of written law.

In Gaul north of the kingdom of Toulouse, Visigothic law also made its impact. First at the court of the Burgundians, for whom we have, at the turn of the fifth and sixth centuries, the *Lex Burgundionum* of King Gundobad, commonly called the *Lex Gundobada*.[61] Like Rothari, Gundobad is concerned, among other things, to enumerate those acts of private violence that could lead to feud between kindreds, and by establishing suitable penalties (often monetary compositions) to check the consequences of bloodshed or damage at an early stage. In general, his matter is very like that of the Kentish laws, though the order is different, and so, too, the penalties. Also like Rothari, Gundobad inserts a king-list, and shows a good deal of interest in the heroic past of his dynasty.[62] Contemporary with

---

[58] These matters are well expounded by Ugo Gualazzini, 'La Scuola Pavese con particolare riguardo all'insegnamento del diritto', *Atti del 4o congresso internazionale di studi sull'Alto Medioevo* (Spoleto, 1969), pp. 35–73. In the *Atti del Io congresso int. di studi longobardi* (1952) will be found an important assessment of Rothari's written sources by E. Besta (pp. 51–69).

[59] *Getica*, ix. 69.

[60] Zeumer, *Neues Archiv*, xxiii, pp. 42 ff., appears to think that they were in the vernacular; so, too, Buchner, *Rechtsquellen*, p. 2.

[61] Ed. de Salis, *MGH Legum* Sect. I, vol. 2 (1892), and F. Beyerle, *Germanenrechte*, x (1936).

[62] On which see Stroheker, 'Studien zu den historisch-geographischen Grundlagen der Nibelungendichtung', *Germanentum und Spätantike*, p. 262.

Gundobad's is the earliest Frankish law—the *Lex Salica*, written near the end of Clovis's reign, with the assistance of Roman lawyers, for all *barbari* under Merovingian rule. Clovis, *rex christianissimus*, produces a wholly pagan code, but produces it apparently in Latin.[63] Some manuscripts (and all are late) contain what are called the Malberg Glosses. These are vernacular words, corrupt but apparently Frankish,[64] that betray either an original Frankish text or the remnants of catch-phrases used by law-speakers or others. Here, too, we find a very long tariff of injuries with appropriate compensations reckoned in money. Unlike Gundobad and Æthelberht, Clovis has no section specially devoted to crimes against the king: he proceeds straight from penalties for failure to attend the *mallus* to fines for stealing animals. But he does include certain scattered provisions affecting his kingship that one might have expected Æthelberht to have adopted if he had had the chance.[65] *Lex Salica* was as active as yeast. The Merovingians who were reigning at about the time of Æthelberht's death or soon after revised it and used it as the basis for a provincial recension known as *Lex Ribvaria*.[66] This was the code that attracted the attention of Jolliffe, though its date precludes it from having been used by Æthelberht. There were also special codes drawn up by the Merovingians for their Alaman and Bavarian subjects before the middle of the seventh century.

I have troubled you with this rather tedious matter the better to make my point that Æthelberht's legislation must be seen in its place among other Germanic laws, and we must suppose that its inspiration was not unlike theirs. He took a decision as did other barbarian kings—and all within a quite short period of time: to have his people's customs written down and attributed

---

[63] Latest ed. by K. A. Eckhardt, in *Germanenrechte, Pactus Legis Salicae, 65 Titel-Text* (Göttingen, 1955).

[64] So R. E. Keller, 'The language of the Franks', *Bulletin of the John Rylands Library*, xlvii (1964).

[65] e.g. 14 (4), 56 (1), and 65 f (4).

[66] Ed. K. A. Eckhardt, *Germanenrechte* (Hanover, 1966), with introductory vol. (1959), and F. Beyerle and R. Buchner, in *MGH Legum* Sect. I, pt. 2 (Hanover, 1954). Frankish law does not stop here. The sixth-century royal edicts were in effect *novellae* to *Lex Salica*. A parallel to Æthelberht cl. 30 is the 596 *decretio* of Childebert II, cl. 5 (*MGH Capit.* i, p. 16).

to him. The political significance of this need not be laboured. But can we make anything more of the interdependence of the barbarian laws? Can we determine what they were for? Plainly they are not law as we find it in the great Roman compilations. Rather, they are a close-knit group of texts deriving from a common source, Roman-Visigothic law. It is entirely uncertain how much of their contents we can accept as accurate statements of current practice, how much was inspired by collections earlier in the queue, and what proportion the scraps that got recorded bear to the whole mass of barbarian custom. For they record, not out of modesty or out of incompetence but simply as a matter of common sense, just that fraction of custom that seemed enough to satisfy royal pride in legislation. This was their immediate practical use. Without for a moment suggesting that their contents were immaterial, or that they cannot be used, with caution, to illustrate social structures, the fact of their existence as books was what mattered most. They recorded customs that were old and new, and sometimes contradictory. Carried about from court to court as a corpus of texts, they must first and foremost have struck their readers as a form of kingly literature. This is why it is so hard to tell to what extent any particular king is concerned to record the ascertainable customs of his people or is content occasionally to attribute to them the customs, already written, of other peoples not unlike his own. A mixture of the two is quite plausible.

To return to Æthelberht's *exempla*: we must accept that Bede and his informants meant what they said by 'iuxta exempla Romanorum'. Though the difference in practice may be slight, I should prefer to understand the phrase, in its context, not as 'after the manner of the Romans', but as 'following Roman patterns or copies'.[67] Which copies, then? Clearly, one candidate must be *Lex Salica*. Sir Frank Stenton, choosing his words with care, states that 'the general affinities [sc. of Æthelberht's law] lie, not with any law-book of the Western Empire, but with the

---

[67] Sir Roger Mynors kindly allows me to say that he considers this an acceptable translation in the present context, and adds that Bede may have avoided *exemplaria*, the word we might expect, because it could have implied that the scribes in Kent actually copied down their barbarian-Roman models— which was not what he thought had happened.

Lex Salica'.[68] He was right: nineteen at least of Æthelberht's ninety chapters do have parallels in *Lex Salica*; and they have a specialized use of a word in common: *leudes*, Kentish *leode*, perhaps aristocratic followers in arms. It may reveal a social rank common to Franks and Kentings; or just possibly one of Augustine's Frankish interpreters may have had a hand in writing down the Kentish vernacular and used an English verbal equivalent of something he was familiar with at home. But *Lex Salica* is only one candidate. There are parallels with Æthelberht's legislation in Burgundian, Gothic, and Lombardic law. The Burgundian link deserves some emphasis. It is a noteworthy fact that the Old English epic poem *Widsith* (seventh-century Mercian as we have it but containing word-forms that betray Kentish origin)[69] preserves the names of three of the four Burgundian kings cited by Gundobad in his laws as his ancestors. At the least, this suggests some early Kentish interest in the Burgundians, from whom, in the sixth century, not only law but also heroic poetry was disseminated, and this despite the fact that their native dynasty was overthrown by the Franks.[70] It also suggests Kentish interest of a general kind in the heroic past of the Germans. Æthelberht's own father, King Eormenric, bore a name famous in Germanic legend. To return to the laws: the fact is that barbarian laws, like barbarian artefacts, are much the same all over the West, and it is well-nigh impossible to tell who is borrowing from whom. The Merovingians could, of course, as part of their general assistance to Pope Gregory, have contributed a copy of *Lex Salica* to his missionaries' travelling library; but, had they done so, the gift could have been politically unwelcome in Kent. On their way to Kent, the missionaries passed through Marseilles, Arles, Vienne, Autun, Tours, and Paris—all cities associated, at one time or another, with the collection or teaching of law.[71] To Autun or to Arles Augustine

---

[68] *Anglo-Saxon England*, p. 60.
[69] Cf. Kemp Malone, ed. *Widsith* (*Anglistica*, xiii, 1962, esp. p. 113; see also pp. 154 ff.).
[70] Cf. Stroheker, 'Nibelungendichtung', pp. 246–74.
[71] On which see P. Riché, 'Enseignement du droit en Gaule du VIᵉ au XIᵉ siècle', *Ius Romanum Medii Aevi*, pt. i, 5b (Milan, 1965), and F. Wieacker, 'Allgemeine Zustände und Rechtszustände gegen Ende des weströmischen Reichs', ibid., pt. i, 2a (Milan, 1963).

went back to be consecrated bishop, and need not have returned empty-handed. From any of these cities the missionaries could have collected legal texts (*exempla*) to add to any texts they had brought from Italy. Such texts would have been accurately described as *exempla Romanorum*. If the missionaries themselves were the *Romani* of Bede's phrase, we should still be left with precisely the same texts from which to select their *exempla*.

The bringing of *exempla* witnessed the link that existed in Roman minds between conversion and law; it was so in Gaul, in Spain, and in Italy; and certainly in Kent. But, with one exception, we shall look in vain for any sign of Christianity among the customs that Æthelberht permitted to be written by his authority. Nor should it be expected.[72] The influence of the Church on barbarian law, after the initial effort of getting it written down, was slow to show itself. It makes no immediate impact on Germanic criminal law or on the law of property and even in matrimonial law is slow and uncertain in its advance. Equally hesitant is its influence on the king's conception of his own authority.[73] Even so late as the laws of Ine, Christian influence is fairly narrowly definable. Early Germanic written law records a selection of customs: it does not consequentially alter them. It reveals, too, the basis of traditional Germanic kingship.

Æthelberht's laws survive in a single manuscript, the Rochester text of the early twelfth century,[74] itself a copy of a Canterbury manuscript of the early eleventh century, if Liebermann is right.[75] The rubric is not original, though it may embody material from a prologue (now lost) such as was common in the continental laws. It might also, on continental analogy, have contained a Kentish king-list. It is a small collection—small

---

[72] Cf. Richardson and Sayles, *Law and Legislation*, pp. 3 ff.

[73] Jean Imbert, 'L'influence du christianisme sur la législation des peuples francs et germains', *Settimane di Studio*, xiv, p. 367, is struck by the influence of the Church on Æthelberht's laws; not so H. Würdinger, 'Einwirkungen des Christentums auf das angelsächsische Recht', *Zeitsch. der Sav. Stift., Germ. Abt.* lxviii (1935), who draws attention to the continued recognition of bride-purchase in cl. 77, on which see Lorraine Lancaster, 'Kinship in Anglo-Saxon society', I, *British Journal of Sociology*, ix. 3 (1958), sect. 3.

[74] Facsimile ed. by P. Sawyer, *Early English Manuscripts in Facsimile*, vols. 7 and 11 (Copenhagen, 1957, 1962).

[75] *Die Gesetze der Angelsachsen*, i (Halle, 1898), p. xxvii. Sawyer, *Text. Roff.* 7, p. 19, thinks that Liebermann was probably right.

enough to make some believe that we have it in truncated form. This I do not accept. It strikes me as a coherent and well-ordered document, such as might be expected from the entourage of Augustine. By and large, what survives is what Æthelberht approved. It is in the vernacular. The obvious explanation for this is that the vernacular was what people understood, and would tend to emphasize Jutish dominance over the mixed population of Kent. Custom must long since have been recited in the vernacular throughout the western world, England included. The point has been made by Professor Whitelock that although 'there is no evidence that the English possessed . . . an official law-speaker . . . it is worth noting that a poem known as *The Gifts of Men* enumerates among the men whom an all-wise Deity endows with special faculties one who "knows the laws, where men deliberate" as well as one who "can in the assembly of wise men determine the custom of the people"'.[76] A selection of written customs as restricted as Æthelberht's would in any case have been of limited practical use. There can be no difficulty in supposing that Augustine and his followers could soon have learnt enough English, at first with the help of Frankish interpreters, to be in a position to write it for the formal purposes of law or charters; and, for myself, I think it quite likely that they had before them, for general guidance as to format, copies of more than one of the continental Germanic laws.

Æthelberht starts off with a famous clause that protects the Church, its property, and its officers against theft and breach of the peace with compensations startlingly heavy. Later, when the pope heard about them, he insisted that simple restitution was all that should be claimed.[77] He was not against compensation as such, and he had nothing to say on the subject of what proportion a bishop's value should bear to a king's. (It is worth noting that Æthelberht's laws provide a very early instance of Church–State parallelism in ranks.)[78] Æthelberht was ready to allow that theft of his bishop's property should bear an elevenfold compensation whereas for himself he was content with ninefold, like

[76] *The Beginnings of English Society* (1952), p. 135.
[77] *Reg.* xi. 56a; Bede, *Hist. Eccl.* i. 27.
[78] As noted by E. H. Kantorowicz, *Laudes Regiae* (Berkeley, 1946), p. 61, n. 164.

the Visigoths. This is not incredible in a newly-converted kingdom, although there are no exact parallels in continental law. Perhaps the ninefold compensation was already customary, perhaps also the elevenfold compensation reflected the protection afforded to a pagan high-priest. Whatever the explanation, the clause should not be considered an interpolation of a later age.

We come next to (what is notably lacking in *Lex Salica*) a group of eleven clauses that involve the king himself. Three of these affect the king's relation to his freemen[79]—protecting him from robbery by them (4), according him a payment for the killing of a freeman involving his own rights (6), and a fine or the confiscated goods when one freeman robbed another (9). A further five (2, 7, 10, 11, 12) protect his servants and followers; and two ensure his own security, dignity, and perhaps sanctity (3, 5). His *mundbyrd* is fixed at fifty shillings (8). Altogether it is not much, and probably not new. Nothing is said of specifically royal occasions such as battle-array or religious functions, nothing of the royal kindred or of royal succession (which so much exercised the minds of the seventh-century Visigoths). One may suspect that Æthelberht has been content to select what made sense to him from among the *exempla* read out to him by his advisers, and to build on that. An overshadowing consideration affecting not only this group of clauses but also the much longer central group (13–72) is the function of feud. Why did Æthelberht and his continental contemporaries devote the bulk of their legislation to detailed and lengthy tariffs of compensation for personal injury and loss or damage of personal property? If we are to trust the barbarian laws at all, we must accept that they apply to societies dominated by feud: that is, to societies of kindreds who could be held responsible for injury done by or to their members. The clash of loyalty between the claims of kindred and those of lordship is a commonplace of Old English literature, and no one would deny nowadays that lordship was an early and vital element in the structure of English society. But there was also a clash within kin-groups. Behind lordship lurk kin-groups arranged in special and by no means uniform ways to settle

---

[79] It should be added that Kent was not peculiarly or predominantly a land of freemen, as Jolliffe believed. I agree with H. P. R. Finberg, 'Roman and Saxon Withington', now in *Lucerna* (1964), p. 64.

differences by feud. It is long before an official voice is raised in Europe to urge that feuding is morally wrong, even though a stigma attached to killing in the opinion of the compilers of private penitentials. Feud could, however, be materially destructive; and it is for this reason that the earliest records of Germanic society show that composition and compensation were as integral a part of the feuding process as the shedding of blood. The point was made by Tacitus. Compositions were not new to Kent when King Æthelberht legislated, though money-compositions may not have been so very old. There must always have been present what social anthropologists call 'the peace within the feud':[80] that is, the inevitable tendency of neighbouring kindreds to settle their differences at an early stage sooner than endure the loss of life or mutilation and destruction of property that would otherwise ensue. It was the sanction of bloodshed that made this possible. Composition by the kindred was an expensive alternative, sometimes too expensive and occasionally even inadmissible. There are instances of this last when a life had been taken. Æthelberht's clause 30 reads 'if one man slays another, he shall pay the wergeld with his own money and property'; and thus his kin was not merely exempted but actually forbidden to intervene, at least as bankers. I doubt if this reflects royal intention to limit feud so much as royal resolve to have done with kin-payments in a particular situation where it had become difficult to decide quickly who *were* the responsible kin. Feuds arose from tiny beginnings. One can imagine a Kentish kindred of Æthelberht's day gladly finding four shillings for the loss of a finger rather than face a running fight that could develop seriously.[81] Even thirty shillings for a severe wound might be worth it if, on Frankish analogy, the payment were shared between the immediate family, father's kin, and mother's kin.[82]

[80] See M. Gluckman, 'The peace in the feud', *Past and Present*, viii (1955).

[81] Liebermann's comment on cl. 54 (i) (*Gesetze*, iii, p. 11) is: 'Mindestens hierin waren die Gliederbussentafeln, bei vielen Völkern, wohl nur juristische Theorie.'

[82] See Maitland's general comments on what a feud-group was, in 'The Laws of Wales: the kindred and the bloodfeud', *Collected Papers*, i, esp. p. 225. L. Lancaster, 'Kinship', i, p. 234, shows how difficult it is to determine what the wider kin was; and further, on the changing meanings of 'agnate' and 'cognate', D. A. Bullough, 'Early medieval social groupings', *Past and Present*, xlv (1969).

In the nature of things these petty differences must usually have involved neighbouring kins who had some members in common; and these would be well to the fore in urging settlement by composition as a merciful escape from the embarrassment of conflicting loyalties. It may not be chance that the classic feud, involving bloodshed over generations, of Uhtred and Thurbrand,[83] was between important families who were not near neighbours; yet even then composition was attempted. Its complicated course is strangely paralleled by that of the equally famous Frankish feud between Sichar and Chramnesind.[84] I find it difficult to credit that 'it was probably more customary for a feud to follow its course' because 'a violent age settled its problems violently',[85] or because the alternative was generally too expensive; for this makes it hard to make sense of the laws themselves, and also goes against the tendency to settlement implicit in the feuding process.[86] It was because the age was violent that another way had to be found, more particularly when a people had reached the end of its migration and was settled on good farming land that nobody wished to see laid waste.

King Æthelberht accepts this situation, for himself and for his people. The king's concern is with peace as much as with war. It had long been so. He and his agents envisage no difficulty in covering the ground. They were presumably available to take the fine when one freeman robbed another; and though it is not stated, we can suppose that royal agents were already being used, as on the continent, to act as arbitrators, and as something more when malefactors moved about the countryside and were inaccessible to any but the king. The king is not consciously limiting the free play of feud for those many occasions when it is still the best solution; nor has he any moral objection to it. Rather, he supplements the procedure where it fails, and perhaps makes something out of it for himself. When all is said, the Kentish laws do reveal a little of contemporary practice. They reveal but

---

[83] Symeon of Durham, *Opera* (Rolls Series), i, pp. 218–19.

[84] Gregory of Tours, *Lib. Hist.* vii. 47 and ix. 19.

[85] H. R. Loyn, *Anglo-Saxon England and the Norman Conquest* (1962), p. 206.

[86] I may refer generally to my discussion in 'The bloodfeud of the Franks', in *The Long-Haired Kings* (1962), pp. 121–47.

do not create it; and they place it under the king's name. For these are the decrees which King Æthelberht established. They are royal *edicta*, not less but more so when approved by his wise men. What is new is that the king, by causing them to be written, makes them his own. Lawgiving is a royal function; it is something that the emperors, through the Church, can give kings. It comes with Christianity. A royal book is made, to be stored, it may be, with the books of the Bible—not inappropriately, either, since the Bible, too, was a repository of law. It is not a book that many will want or could use. There will have been few copies. Æthelberht's successors add to the collection, each appropriating the whole as his own law. What have they gained with their law-books? They have really issued a modest political manifesto. It binds together, as the new religion also binds together, the mixed peoples of Kent under a royal authority. Exactly the same process can be seen in Visigothic Spain under the great king Liuvigild;[87] and there, too, the king does not get very far without exciting opposition. Liuvigild's subjects reacted against his Arianism, in favour of Catholicism; Æthelberht's, against his Catholicism, in favour of paganism. Their laws remained, however.

Æthelberht's death was followed by apostasy. But paganism had nothing fresh to offer a seventh-century king: only the solace of what was old. Æthelberht's pagan ancestry mattered to his Christian advisers: why not to him? In a masterly paper,[88] Dr. Kenneth Sisam showed how little trust could be placed in the early parts of the surviving genealogies of the Anglo-Saxon kings. As we have them, they reflect eighth-century Mercian interest in genealogy. However, a written genealogy that relates each king to his predecessor is not the same as a simple king-list; nor does its absence from early documents exclude the inherent likelihood that kings were interested in their ancestry. Christian kings could hardly escape the influence of biblical genealogies, not least of Christ's own genealogy. An out-of-the-way Frankish bishop such as Maurilio of Cahors could repeat the Old Testament genealogies by heart, which, adds Gregory of Tours, few can

[87] Cf. Stroheker, 'Leowigild', *Germanentum und Spätantike*, p. 162.
[88] 'Anglo-Saxon royal genealogies', *Proc. Brit. Acad.* xxxix (1953).

memorize.[89] I am not quite so sceptical as Dr. Sisam is about
Bede's Kentish king-list, brief and schematic though it be. That
Æthelberht liked to represent himself as descended from Woden
is plausible enough, surely. His people would have expected it,
for, in Stenton's phrase, 'there must have been a strong basis of
popular feeling beneath the aristocratic convention which regarded Woden as the ancestor of most English kings'.[90] A hereditary claim, even backed by a genealogy such as Æthelberht's, was
a 'sure earnest of a successful reign', and 'if royal blood did not
exist it could be discovered'.[91] What is more, Æthelberht was
married to a Merovingian princess, who had become his wife
while he was still a minor.[92] In no family was hereditary descent
more strictly observed and buttressed than in the Merovingian.
Gregory the Great himself emphasized the point that Frankish
kingship was hereditary.[93] If he took little else from his formidable connections, Æthelberht would surely have learned how to
make the most of his blood. There were missionaries at hand to
see that he did it. One cannot rule out the possibility that a copy
of Gregory of Tours' Frankish history was already available in
Canterbury before Æthelberht's death. The missionaries had
visited Tours, where the great bishop had died not long before;
and Canterbury seems the likeliest place from which, belatedly,
Bede obtained some knowledge of Gregory's writings. The
Frankish history, for all its criticism of Merovingian kings who
had been Æthelberht's contemporaries, exalts the power of
Clovis, the first Catholic Merovingian, and attributes his victories
to his new religion. Æthelberht was a Kentish, if not an English,
Clovis. His very success will have made him think of Christianity
—not necessarily as an exclusive religion but as a useful addition
to his pantheon of a god particularly associated with recent victories on the continent. It was safe to take Christ from Rome, if
not from Paris. Whether he thought it had been worthwhile, in
the end, we cannot tell; his laws give us no clue. But laws he got;

[89] *Hist. Lib.* v. 42.
[90] 'The historical bearing of place-name studies', p. 20.
[91] Loyn, *Anglo-Saxon England*, p. 204.
[92] Gregory of Tours, *Hist. Lib.* iv. 26 and ix. 26.
[93] *Hom. in Evang.* x, c. 5 (*Pat. Lat.* lxxvi, col. 1112). This was cited in c. 1
of the *Libellus proclamationis adversus Wenilonem* of 859 (*MGH Capit.* ii,
p. 450).

and a new fighting purpose with a promise of victory; and a mythology more powerful than any the pagans knew; and an assured place in the Christian kingdom of heaven. It was a good gamble, at least. His steps were hesitant, and taken rather for himself than for his people: it was for him that Christ might be useful, if not paraded too much before his notoriously pagan countrymen. The pope thought him slow off the mark and too reluctant to compel conversion. It was a mistake that Gregory made on other occasions. Æthelberht went too far, in the short run. But in the long run, his dynasty survived in large measure because of the advantages it owed to conversion. Christianity made for dynastic permanence. Those dynasties that survived the seventh century in England and abroad had become Christian.

III

THE SEVENTH CENTURY

A CHANGE in emphasis comes over western kingship in the seventh century; kings move into an ecclesiastical atmosphere; they are required to consider their duties in a fresh light, and may actually have done so. It is not that the Church has evolved and can present a clear doctrine of kingship. The position is rather that churchmen, here and there, in widely differing circumstances, are ready to make claims on kings—claims that move roughly in the same direction. One reason for their lack of unanimity is plain: the Bible furnished them with many instances of kingship in action, good and bad, but from these they had to draw their own conclusions. And they found another difficulty, a contradiction in the Bible which they expressed in their teaching: on the one hand, the idea of God as king in his kingdom of heaven, the head of a hierarchy that had its counterpart on earth, and, on the other, the idea of the equality of all men before God.[1] Gregory the Great saw the difficulty and felt that on the whole subordination to one's proper superiors overruled the claims of natural equality; 'regia dignitas', he told King Childebert, 'takes precedence of any other man's'.[2] He was not explicit on the reasons for this; but he said enough to give a strong lead to the thinkers of the ninth century.[3] Kings, then, could have their place in the hierarchy of good order; but also they could block man's path to a common Christian equality.

---

[1] This point is developed in an interesting way by F. X. Graus, *Volk, Herrscher und Heiliger im Reich der Merowinger* (Prague, 1965), pp. 304 ff.

[2] *Reg.* vi, 6, p. 384.

[3] On this see the illuminating comments of Walter Ullmann, *The Carolingian Renaissance and the Idea of Kingship* (1969), pp. 114 ff., and *The Individual and Society in the Middle Ages*, pp. 14 ff., where attention is also drawn to the effects on Hincmar's hierarchical thinking of Pseudo-Dionysius, then recently translated into Latin by John Scotus Eriugena.

The thinkers of the seventh century saw the problem but could not solve it; they spoke with too many voices. Yet as a rule they tended to speak in a way favourable to kingly power, both in England and on the continent.

The first half of the seventh century was, in Francia, the golden age of Merovingian rule. Two kings at least—Chlotar II and his son Dagobert I—showed plainly that they believed their power to be God-given and also (though not consequentially) an instrument for the protection of the Church. It was their duty to assist the good and punish the wicked—in technical terms, to further *iustitia* or *aequitas*.[4] King Gunthram, a little earlier, had expressed it thus: 'Convenit ergo, ut iustitiae et aequitatio in omnibus vigore servato distringat legalis ultio iudicum.'[5] The correlative of *iustitia* was *pietas*; and royal *pietas* was more than personal. It involved the protection of doctrine and morals, of the poor and of the churches themselves, their officers and their possessions. Why kings should have accepted this interpretation of their role is not at once obvious. Fredegar reports that what was noteworthy about Chlotar II was his *pietas* and his *patientia*;[6] and in the preface to the canons of the council of Clichy the same king was compared with David.[7] This is the first known Frankish instance of what was to become a commonplace. Moreover, his office is called a 'ministrationem propheticam'; he must protect the Church that protects him. The accession of his son Dagobert was welcomed by Fredegar in well-nigh biblical terms, as the advent of the rule of righteousness; indeed, Fredegar says the king was so busy doing justice that he scarcely had time to eat or sleep, and even had to conduct business in his bath.[8] Not much later, he is compared with Solomon, the *rex pacificus*.[9] The fact is, that Chlotar and Dagobert were as bloodthirsty as their predecessors and had their full share of troubles; but it still made sense to emphasize these dimly realized ideals, and to tie them to a biblical past. Dagobert's son, Clovis II, was

[4] I here largely follow Eugen Ewig's brilliant summary in *Das Königtum*, pp. 19 ff.
[5] *MGH Capit.* i, p. 12, nr. 5.
[6] *Hist.* iv. 42.
[7] *MGH Conc.* i, p. 196.
[8] *Hist.* iv. 58.
[9] *Liber Historiae Francorum*, 42.

the recipient of a letter of admonition, urging upon him the examples of David and Solomon, warning him to listen to his bishops, advising him to consider the careers of his predecessors and listing the kingly virtues that were expected of him; let him be careful about his advisers: 'nullus potest esse fidelis regi cuius sermo non stat', and so forth. Only thus can he hope to reign long and luckily.[10] Not all of this was new; but clearly the assumption is made that the king's moral duties are Christian duties as interpreted by his Church. It is not easy to distinguish the *minister Dei* from the *minister ecclesiae*. The mid-seventh-century formulary of Marculf contains pieces of the same complexion. A *preceptum de episcopatum* summons the king 'ad ministrandum gubernandumque rerum statu(m)';[11] he governs his kingdom and he ministers to his Church. In another *carta* he is God's representative for earthly rule.[12] In others he must bestow *iudiciaria potestas* only upon those of proved *fides* and *strenuitas*.[13] He must exercise *deliberatio*[14] and be ready with his *largitas* in the right quarters.[15] One could construct a kind of mirror of princes from the *arengae* of Marculf's charters alone. It is useless to inquire how literally any of this was taken; but it is there; and by no means all of it would have seemed foreign or absurd to warrior-kings.

The same message is elaborated in the Gallican liturgies of the seventh and early eighth centuries. The Autun sacramentary offers prayers for royal *pax, concordia,* and *pietas*;[16] that of Auxerre associates the peace of the Church with the victory of Christian kings over the heathen;[17] and in the palimpsest of Reichenau the Franks are identified with the people of Israel.[18] In other words, the Frankish Church is turning the warlike aspect of kingship to its own uses: you cannot stop kings fighting but you can encourage them to fight the right enemies; and in

[10] *MGH Epist.*, pp. 457–60.
[11] *MGH Form., Legum* Sect. V, p. 45. Reference should also be made to the texts in Alf Uddholm, *Marculfi Formularum Libri Duo* (Uppsala, 1962).
[12] Ibid., p. 109.
[13] Ibid., p. 47.
[14] Ibid., p. 58.
[15] Ibid., pp. 52, 64, 66.
[16] Ewig, *Das Königtum*, p. 23.
[17] Ibid.
[18] Ibid.

the Old Testament parallel of Israel you can identify still more closely with the purposes of the Church. The Bobbio missal contains a *missa pro principe*, probably Merovingian in origin, which invokes God's help for kings and accepts the divine institution of kingship, royal responsibility for peace and for war against the heathen, and the solidarity of king and people at prayer.[19] Prayers for the Merovingians seem in general to be fairly specific in their requirements and are not the vague, impersonal utterances we have been taught to expect.[20] One can only conclude that, in the seventh century, Merovingian kings were looked at in a very different way from that sketched by Einhard in the ninth century. One would be hard put to it to discern any clearly heathen element in the kingship of Chlotar and Dagobert. The careers of such rulers could be fitted, not too uncomfortably, into the framework of a church-historiography, and their bodies could be buried sumptuously in the churches of the saints with whom they had chosen to connect their good fortune in life. The abbey-church of St. Denis, near Paris, was particularly favoured by the Merovingians, especially since the time of its great benefactor, Dagobert, who was buried there. Dagobert's tomb no longer survives, nor that of any of his house except Aunegundis, queen of Chlotar I, who died about 570.[21] Her undisturbed grave, only recently excavated, contained her limestone coffin, traces of her embalmed body, shreds of fine clothing and much jewellery. Also, it contained her inscribed gold ring, which is why we can identify her. Apart from 'a single glass bottle wrapped in a white cloth', her coffin contained none of the knick-knacks and sustenance associated with earlier graves. There was nothing ritually pagan about her burial; she was a Christian princess. One supposes that the male Merovingians were buried in the same manner.

Perhaps it is surprising that the Merovingians' close connection with the shrines of saints and the dens of holy men should not have led to a widespread cultus of holy kings, such as we find

[19] Ewig, *Das Königtum*, p. 24. Ewig accepts the position that the *missa* belongs to the thought-world of the seventh century but was developed by the early Carolingians.

[20] As by C. A. Bouman, *Sacring and Crowning* (Groningen, 1957), pp. 92–3.

[21] See the provisional report by Joachim Werner, 'Frankish royal tombs in the cathedrals of Cologne and Saint-Denis', *Antiquity*, xxxviii (1964), pp. 203 ff.

with the Carolingians and the English. However, there are
signs in the huge corpus of Frankish saints' Lives that something of the sort was beginning.[22] It is always hard to say what
royal attributes should be termed charismatic or how important
they were to the idea of kingship. What weight, for example,
should be allowed to Fredegar's sea-beast story? And is it significant that Gregory of Tours, for all his interest in kingship, said
nothing about the story? Whatever was useful or had *strenuitas*
about the Merovingian pagan heritage had been subsumed into
a new kind of kingship, carefully adapted to find room for it; but
royal charisma, when it does appear, is firmly linked to the Bible,
not with sea-beasts. When Gregory tells of the thaumaturgical
power of King Gunthram, he sees it as a Christian power; his
Gunthram is a Church-king—indeed, almost a bishop when he
tries. We have to bear in mind that the influential men among
the Frankish bishops and abbots (as elsewhere) were mostly of
aristocratic birth. They would have been unlikely to tolerate an
interpretation of royal rule that was unfavourable to practical
authority, or in any way sceptical. Kings could be castigated for
their shortcomings, but kingship needed bolstering. Indeed, they
show a tendency to attribute failure or inadequacy in high office
to low birth, as was markedly the case with certain queens. The
Lives of the Frankish saints reflect this approach. Obedience and
fidelity to kings are right and natural, and rebellion, so far from
being justifiable, is seen as the fruit of pride. Blame for bad rule
is better attributed to the royal entourage than to kings themselves, at least in the first instance. On the whole, what might
be called anti-royal sentiment is far less marked in Frankish
saints' Lives than in the *acta martyrum* and eremetical Lives
that were the models for the Frankish hagiographers. This is
not to say that kings were rated higher than saints in the Frankish scale of social values but only that the world in which the
saints operated depended upon good rule—that is, upon kings
who accepted and protected them. One king who did this whole-
heartedly took pains to say so; for the Life of Desiderius of
Vienne was written by no less a man than Sisebut, king of the
Visigoths.[23] There are occasions when holy men humiliate or

[22] This is argued by Graus in *Volk, Herrscher und Heiliger, passim.*
[23] *MGH Script. Rer. Mero.* iii, pp. 620–48.

punish kings, foretell royal catastrophies, and intervene to stop battles; and naturally they protect church property against marauding kings, notably through miracles. All this needs no explanation and detracts not at all from the general feeling of reverence for kings. Occasionally someone of royal blood will himself achieve holiness, usually by renunciation of rule or by what is later represented as martyrdom. Examples of this are St. Chlodowald, St. Sigismund,[24] and the Visigoth Hermenigild, though with all three sanctity is not associated with their practice of kingship. Dagobert may possibly have been the subject of a cultus fairly soon after his death,[25] and to writers of a later generation seemed to have been an ideal king. A few other Merovingians achieved a belated sanctity: Dagobert's son, Sigibert III, was one such, and Sigibert's son, Dagobert II, another. We shall see that the Anglo-Saxon kings did rather better than this. By the seventh century, three former Merovingian queens were considered holy: Chrotechildis, queen of Clovis, who had played some part in his conversion; Ultragotha, queen of Childebert I;[26] and Radegundis, queen of Chlotar I, an ascetic and a monastic founder, with her own cult in Poitiers.[27] But the most notable was Balthildis, queen of Clovis II, mother of several kings and regent for one of them. Balthildis had come to Francia as an English slave. Her rise to power and exercise of it could certainly not be called holy; indeed, the best moral trait that her hagiographer could find in her was the *humilitas* which she owed to her origins. Nevertheless, she had been a great supporter of churches and monasteries, had forbidden the export of slaves and had lightened taxes; and these could be dressed up as specifically royal traits of holiness. Her public character mattered. These are the traits that we find in her biography, written soon after her death as part of her cultus at Chelles.[28] No later Merovingian queen achieved this status—or not, at any rate, till Carolingian times.

[24] See R. Folz, 'La légende liturgique de saint Sigismond d'après un manuscrit d'Agaune', *Speculum Historiale* (Munich), pp. 152–66.
[25] See Folz, 'Tradition hagiographique et culte de saint Dagobert, roi des Francs', *Le Moyen Âge, livre jubilaire* (1963), pp. 17–35.
[26] See, for example, on these, *Vita Balthildis*, ch. 18 (*MGH Script. Rer. Mero.* ii, pp. 505–6).
[27] *Vita Radegundis*, ibid., pp. 358–95.
[28] Ibid., pp. 482–58.

In brief, then, Frankish respect for the Merovingians never reached the point where it was possible to expect or assume royal sanctity; but the beginnings of expectation are there; and certainly no Frankish hagiographer found any charisma of pagan kingship that was of much use to him.

The Visigoths thought harder about kingship, and that not only in the context of biblical kingship. They had an eye to imperial example, since parts of Spain were still held by Byzantine troops. The Visigoth view of kingship was most fully elaborated by Isidore of Seville—so fully, indeed, that one can do no more than sketch its outlines. Isidore was no hagiographer but a political thinker in whose writings is a consistent picture of kingship as he saw it developing in Gothic history. It was central to his idea of a Christian state; that is to say, of a Germanic *regnum gentis* independent of emperors, secure within the *regnum Christi*, and coterminous with Spain. His ideal king exercises *potestas* over his people and within his national church;[29] and it should be real *potestas*, characterized by *virtus* and by *terror disciplinae*.[30] Behind this lay the famous distinction of Pope Gelasius; but Isidore goes further. He holds that the king's *potestas* exists not independently of the Church but in order to protect it and further its purpose:[31] 'reges a recte agendo vocati sunt, ideoque recte faciendo regis nomen tenetur, peccando amittetur.'[32] A king who fails to rule in the right way is no king but a tyrant. Not that his Church can do anything about it; he must be accepted by his people as a punishment for their sins. There is no machinery for getting rid of him. His special duty is to make, administer, and obey law; and obey he can and should if, like David, he shows *humilitas*.[33] The virtues he must cultivate are *iustitia* and *pietas*, the one tempering the other.[34] Isidore is

---

[29] *Sententiae*, iii. 51 (*Pat. Lat.*, lxxxiii, col. 723).

[30] Ibid.

[31] Ibid. Compare the words of Pope Gelasius: 'Duo quippe sunt, imperator auguste, quibus principaliter mundus hic regitur: auctoritas sacrata pontificum et regalis potestas. In quibus tanto gravius est pondus sacerdotum, quanto etiam pro ipsis regibus hominum in divino reddituri sunt examine rationem' (*Epist.* xii. 2).

[32] *Sent.* iii. 48 (*Pat. Lat.* lxxxiii, col. 719), and *Etymologiae*, ix. 4.

[33] *Sent.* iii. 49 (*Pat. Lat.* lxxxiii, col. 720).

[34] *Etymol.* ix. 3, 5.

quite clear, then, that kingship is the exercise of a Christian function, and that what the king holds is neither more nor less than a *ministerium*, an office, within the Church. Because a king knows how to rule himself, he is also equipped to rule and correct his subjects; not otherwise. This sounds as if kingship as traditionally understood by the barbarians is being circumscribed and reduced. But if one looks at Isidore's account of recent Visigoth kings in his Gothic History[35] one gets a very different impression; for he delights in the Gothic unification of Spain, the defeats of the imperial armies and the military exploits of successive kings. He has no patience with the rebellious Hermenigild and is full of praise for Liuvigild's reign of military suppression, leading, as it did, to the Catholic conversion of his son, Reccared. But Reccared, too, was a fighter, replete with all the right virtues, 'so that he seems not so much to have waged wars as to have trained his people'. Much the same could be said of the learned Sisebut, Isidore's own patron, and of Swinthila, who 'is worthy to be called not only the ruler of peoples but the father of the poor'. The future of Spain was assured under such rulers. This in practice was what Isidore meant by *iustitia* and *pietas*, and one begins to see why the kings in question felt no diminution of their authority when cast as agents of the Church, but rather an increase. They were acquiring a role that did not replace something they had before but was an addition that went a long way towards giving them a justifiable occupation in peace as well as war.

Isidore was not speculating in a vacuum. He was an active and extremely influential bishop. The effect of his thinking is clear in the politics of seventh-century Spain and beyond. Before its close, there were manuscripts of some of his writings in northern Francia,[36] and their subsequent dissemination was very rapid. The fourth council of Toledo, in 633, whose canons may have been drafted by Isidore personally,[37] designates the king *minister*

---

[35] *MGH Auct. Ant.* xi, chs. 49–70.

[36] See Bernhard Bischoff, 'Die europäische Verbreitung der Werke Isidors von Sevilla', in *Mittelalterliche Studien*, i (Stuttgart, 1966).

[37] Cf. Ewig, *Das Königtum*, pp. 34–7. The Toledan conciliar view of the king's office is also discussed by F. Kern, *Gottesgnadentum und Widerstandsrecht* (ed. Buchner, Münster, 1954), esp. p. 47, n. 98.

Dei and insists on his *iustitia* and *pietas*.[38] Royal accessions are no longer to be determined in an atmosphere of barbarian shield-banging but through the *commune consilium* of the great, lay and spiritual. The royal oath will be a divinely-sanctioned *pactum* between king and people, guaranteed by the Church. When we move on to the eighth council, twenty years later, royal *iustitia* and *pietas* are reinforced by *veritas, misericordia,* and *pax*;[39] the procedure for royal accessions is worked out in more detail; the royal function ,of law-giving is further clarified 'regem etenim iura faciunt, non persona, quia nec constat sui medio-critate sed sublimitatis honore.' The office of king is thus an *honor* in the sense of *ministerium*. The king who presided over this council and published its decrees was Reccaswinth. A pro-vincial synod at Merida, in 666, decreed that daily masses should be said for him, his followers, and his army, together with prayers for victory over his enemies.[40] This is an exact parallel to the Frankish *missa pro principe*. Reccaswinth was also author of the most important of all the royal revisions of Gothic law, the *Forum Iudicum*. In this, too, the influence of Isidore is plain. It states that laws, enacted with *consensus universalis* for the *communis utilitas* and binding on kings, ensure internal peace and victory over external enemies.[41] It defines kingship in terms borrowed from Isidore and the Toledan decrees; and it does what it can to interpret Roman *laesa maiestas* in terms of Christian *infidelitas*. After Reccaswinth we reach Wamba, the first Gothic king to receive unction. There indeed we enter a different world, but one that would have been inconceivable without a century of close collaboration between the Visigothic kings and their clerical friends.

An influence upon kingship that I have not yet mentioned is that of the Irish, and I have left it till now because it forms a convenient link between the continent and England. The Irish law-tracts of the sixth and seventh centuries betray a kingship

[38] *Pat. Lat.* lxxxiv, cols. 385 ff.
[39] Ibid., cols. 417 ff.
[40] Ibid., col. 616c, d. With this one may associate the sentiment of the *Ordo quando rex ad prelium egreditur*, which is Visigothic and approximately con-temporary, ed. M. Férotin, *Le Liber Ordinum, Monumenta Ecclesiae Liturgica,* v (Paris, 1904), cols. 149–53.
[41] *Lex Visigot. Recceswinth.* i. 2, 6.

still pagan in important respects. It is sacral, bound up with luck and disaster. In a saga attached to one law-tract it matters that the king should be physically perfect. Initiation ceremonies signify, as they must long have done, the king's marriage with the tribal goddess.[42] An Irish contemporary, or near-contemporary, of Isidore wrote a tract of another kind, known as the *de duodecim abusivis saeculi*.[43] His eighth abuse, the *rex iniquus*, and to a slight extent his seventh, the *dominus sine virtute*,[44] form a mirror of princes more deliberate than Marculf's Frankish pieces. The princely shortcomings they enumerate presuppose the qualities that made a good king in Irish eyes. All the same, they hardly constitute a body of thought about the king's role in society such as Isidore attempted. The tract's view of kingship is part-Christian, part-pagan; a traditional view is retained in so far as it is compatible with a Christian society, and a little specifically Christian matter is worked into it. Its king has something old and mythical about him, such as we do not find on the continent. He is 'pax populorum, tutamen patriae . . . munimentum gentis, cura languorum, gaudium hominum, temperies aeris, serenitas maris, terrae fecunditas, solacium pauperum, hereditas filiorum et sibimet ipsi spes futurae beatitudinis'. The Irish king has only to go wrong to cause all sorts of natural catastrophies. No Merovingian of the seventh century was actually reported to have influenced weather or harvest, whatever may have been said at the time; and it is uncertain whether such reports of Carolingian kings (by Alcuin, for example) witnessed to an unbroken Frankish tradition or to the arrival in Francia of the Irish tradition—or to both. Some Old Testament influence on the Irish-

---

[42] I am indebted for information on this point to Professor D. A. Binchy. His *Celtic and Anglo-Saxon Kingship* contains a valuable assessment of the pagan Irish view of kingship. See in particular his treatment of the Testament of Morand (p. 9), which he considers the oldest mirror of princes in western Europe. Its contents strongly suggest that Pseudo-Cyprian (see next footnote) had access to it, or to other material like it.

[43] Ed. S. Hellmann, *Pseudo-Cyprianus, De XII Abusivis Saeculi* (*Texte und Untersuchungen zur Geschichte der altchristlichen Literatur*, 3, Reihe iv, Leipzig, 1910). See also R. Mitchell-Smith, 'The speculum principum in early Irish literature', *Speculum*, ii (1927), pp. 411–55.

[44] It seems to me that Ewig, *Königtum*, p. 40, following Schlesinger, goes too far in equating the *dominus* here with the warrior-king as distinct from the sacral king.

man may be detected here, notably that of Genesis 27:27-9, though curiously not that of the bad king of the Book of Samuel, preferred by the continental writers. Fundamentally, however, the picture is not Christian at all. The writer sees his king as the embodiment of his people's luck and prosperity, not as the holder of a Christian office. His single virtue is *iustitia*, broadly interpreted to embrace such Christian duties as protection of churches, the poor, widows, and foreigners, the suppression of *impietas*, and the upholding of oaths. He must avoid *iracundia*, be on his guard against the moral temptations of prosperity but also of adversity, and must guard his own children against impiety. Directly or not, something of this approach can be glimpsed in the Merovingian world, to some extent in royal responsibility for the legal protection of foreigners, the poor, widows, and orphans.[45] There is also, I suspect, a possibility that the traditional materials from which the tract was constructed affected the approach to kingship of the great Irish missionaries, Columba and Columbanus.

If we may trust Adomnan, writing a century after Columba's death, the saint had something of the attitude to kings that we find in the tract. He is made supernaturally aware of the outcome of royal decisions and is ready to concern himself with royal business. 'In the fearful crash of battles', writes Adomnan, 'Columba obtained through prayer to God that some kings were conquered and others were conquerors. This was a special favour bestowed on him by God, who honours all saints, not only in his lifetime but also after death, as on a triumphant and powerful champion.[46] Adomnan goes on to give an example of this last from the experience of King Oswald. Columba could prophesy the outcome of royal battles being fought at a great distance from him, as, for example, the Irish battle of Ond-móne,[47] and the battle of the Miathi.[48] He could also prophesy that King Roderc would not be slain in battle but would die on his own feather bed.[49] When, on divine instruction, he ordained Aidan king of

[45] As Ewig points out, ibid., p. 41, n. 155. Cf. *MGH Epist. Mero.*, i, p. 113 (*Epist. Aust.* 2) and pp. 457 ff. (*Epist. Mero.* 15).
[46] *Adomnan's Life of Columba*, ed. A. O. and M. O. Anderson (1961), p. 198.
[47] Ibid., p. 224.
[48] Ibid., p. 226.
[49] Ibid., p. 238.

the Dal-Réti by laying on of hands, he also took occasion to prophesy the future of Aidan's son, grandsons, and great-grandsons.[50] And there is a hint of something sterner when the gates of the fortress of the haughty King Brude spontaneously open to him.[51] In brief, Columba, himself of royal stock, shows prophetic concern for the fates of kings, if not directly for their morals. His life is bound up with theirs.

The involvement has increased in the career of Columbanus, who was active in Merovingian Francia in the generation after Columba. In the excellent biography of him written by Jonas of Bobbio,[52] he appears as a holy terror to kings in the true prophetic spirit of the Old Testament. Yet they are fascinated by his special brand of sanctity. They settle him on the land he wants,[53] and often they beg his prayers.[54] But some things they will not take from him. He tells King Theudebert that he ought to become a monk. This is greeted with ridicule: 'se numquam audisse (Merovingum) in regno sublimatum voluntarium clericum fuisse.' 'Well then,' replies Columbanus, 'if you won't do it voluntarily you will do it involuntarily', for he foresees that the king will be defeated in battle and tonsured; which in due course happens. Worse still, he rebukes King Theuderic for his concubines, on the ground that royal progeny should be born of honourable queens.[55] He refuses his blessing to the king's sons so born, though in Merovingian eyes they were none the worse for their mothers. The earth shakes as the saint leaves the royal hall in fury. Naturally enough Theuderic hounded him out of his kingdom. Yet, other Merovingians were still ready to welcome him. King Chlotar even sent to the exile in Bobbio to beg him to return. All he got in reply was 'litteras castigationum'. The Merovingians could take a great deal in the way of stinging

---

[50] *Adomnan's Life of Columba*, ed. A. O. and M. O. Anderson (1961), p. 474. Cf. Ewig, *Königtum*, p. 37.

[51] Ibid., p. 408.

[52] Ed. B. Krusch, *Script. Rer. Germ. in usum schol.* (Hannover, 1905).

[53] Ibid., p. 163.

[54] Ibid., p. 186.

[55] Ibid., pp. 187 ff. Another missionary of the Columbanic tradition, the Frankish-Aquitanian St. Amand, was to refuse baptism to a Merovingian prince because of his father's morals, and was expelled for his pains. *Vita Amandi*, ch. 17 (*MGH, Script. Rer. Mero.*, v, p. 440).

rebuke and moral exhortation from those they protected; but they would not take interference in the succession. Clearly an important stage has been reached when a powerful line of kings, already deeply involved in the protection of churches and shrines, gives a welcome to foreign monks of ascetic stamp, who are not in the least prepared to leave royal morals alone. Somehow the Merovingians felt that the good luck and prosperity of their rule were inseparable from the prayers of saints, living and departed. The Celtic strain of sanctity crystallizes a long-felt Merovingian wish to invoke the patronage of holy men and holy places. Plainly much of the prophetic and miraculous power attributed to the Irishmen belongs to the field of literary hindsight; it was for monastic consumption. Yet Jonas of Bobbio was writing about a man only recently dead. He was putting into words the general impression Columbanus had just been making on the Merovingian court-circle; the political impact of the great Irishman was real enough. Frankish kingship is a little different because of it—even in the days of weakness that lay ahead.

The Merovingians were not alone in feeling the effect of Irish ascetics whose view of kingship came partly from the Old Testament and partly from the pagan background of kingship as they had known it at home in Ireland. Anglo-Saxon kingship was at least as strongly influenced. One thinks at once of Bede, whom I shall leave aside for the present. Bede apart, our English material must in the main be the Lives of saints, less numerous indeed than the Frankish Lives but better in quality, at least as biographies. Two of these, the anonymous Life of Cuthbert and Felix's Life of Guthlac, have much in common, not only in their authors' assumptions about kings but also in their continental models.[56] A third, Æddi's Life of Wilfrid, stands apart. As a group, and in so far as kingship is concerned, they aim to give their readers—communities of monks—a picture of kings who prosper because of their association with saints (whether hermits, monks, nuns, or bishops). Their kings participate in the life of the Church as founders, benefactors, and protectors; and in proportion to their assistance they succeed as kings. It is a picture by

[56] On these see B. Colgrave, 'The earliest saints' lives written in England', *Proc. Brit. Acad.* xliv (1958).

monks and for monks. The surviving manuscripts do not suggest any very wide circulation in the seventh and early eighth centuries. They may be seen as one kind of substitute for heroic literature in monastic communities that contained many of aristocratic and some of royal blood. Because of this specialized background one must discount part of their record as pious invention; what part, is not always easy to say, particularly when a writer or community has been closely associated with a king and continues the association with his kindred. The two circles, royal and monastic, contain important members common to both. We have to consider not only the proportion of factual truth in a royal Life but also what the effect of that Life may be on the king's successors and relations.

The Life of St. Guthlac is conceived as literature for monks. But it is more. Felix addresses his prologue to 'my lord king Ælfwald, beloved to me beyond any other of royal rank, who rules by right over the kingdom of the East Angles. . . . In obedience to your commands . . . I have drawn up the book which you bade me compose concerning the life of our father Guthlac. . . . In this confidence I have publicly presented it to you.'[57] In short, the king will read the book, or hear it read. What sort of man is the king so anxious to hear about? In the first place, Guthlac was himself of royal blood, being related to Ælfwald and descended 'per nobilissima inlustrium regum nomina' from Icel, founder of the dynasty.[58] As a young man he is, inevitably, a war-band leader, until he has a vision of 'the wretched deaths and shameful ends of the ancient kings of his race in the course of the past ages'.[59] So he renounces the secular life, disregarding the reverence due to his royal blood and the prayers of his followers. After a course at Repton, under the abbess Ælfthryth, he ends up in the fens, with St. Bartholomew as ghostly patron. His subsequent career as a solitary is centred upon his own spiritual struggle; and yet, like his continental counterparts, he is not cut off from the affairs of kings. The abbess Ecgburh, daughter of King Aldwulf, has questions for

[57] Ed. B. Colgrave, *Felix's Life of Saint Guthlac* (1956), p. 61 (whose translations I cite).
[58] Ibid., p. 74.
[59] Ibid., p. 83.

him.[60] The exiled Æthelbald of Mercia, hounded by King Ceolred, seeks him out and is comforted by Guthlac's assurance that, at his prayer, God has granted that he shall in the end rule over his kingdom and cut down his enemies: 'not as booty nor as spoil shall the kingdom be granted to you, but you shall obtain it from the hand of God.' And so, of course, it happened, as events proved:[61] 'as times change, generations and kingdoms change too.' In due course King Æthelbald was to surround Guthlac's tomb with 'miris ornamentorum structuris';[62] but before then, while still in exile, he was to seek further reassurance from the dead Guthlac, who appeared to him in a vision and prophesied his imminent success. 'From that time until the present, his happiness as king over his realm has grown daily as year succeeds year.'[63] Certainly it did, for Æthelbald became a powerful king who was not afraid to be the protector of the exiled Wilfrid. Yet there was another side to him. He was the recipient of a curious letter from St. Boniface. It praises his faith in God, his alms-giving, his repression of robbery, perjury, and rapine, his defence of widows and the poor, and gives thanks for the peace and pros-perity of his kingdom; but it castigates his adultery with nuns and his seizure of monastic property, both unforgivable in a king who owed his crown not to his own merits but to God.[64] In fact, once king, Æthelbald had not found it possible to avoid the path of his wicked predecessor, Ceolred. What he gave with one hand he took back with the other. He was equivocal. But this we should not guess from the royal hero of Guthlac's Life, as presented to King Ælfwald by Felix.

Boniface remonstrated with kings. Felix's Guthlac did not: he prophesied and intervened with God for them. Another prophet is St. Cuthbert. His anonymous biographer represents him as a solitary by choice and a bishop by compulsion; a miracle-worker living under the protection of angels. He has no direct mission to kings. The royal abbess Ælfflaed seeks him out to inquire how long her brother, King Ecgfrith of Northumbria,

[60] Ibid., p. 147.
[61] Ibid., pp. 149, 151.
[62] Ibid., p. 162.
[63] Ibid., p. 167.
[64] *MGH Epist. Sel.* i (Berlin, 1955), ed. M. Tangl, no. 73, pp. 146 ff. Boniface appears in this letter to be using the argument of Ps.-Cyprian, *Abusio* 9.

had to live.[65] Twelve months was the answer. And who would succeed him? Aldfrith, then on Iona, who, adds the biographer, 'now reigns peacefully . . . the fall of the members of the royal house by a cruel hand and a hostile sword a year afterwards renewed all the bitterness for her and for many others'. On the day of King Ecgfrith's death at Nechtansmere or Dunnichen Moss, Cuthbert pauses in his tour of the walls of Carlisle to warn his companions of what was even then happening: 'I think that the war is over and that judgement has been given against our people in the battle.'[66] For this was the predestined judgement of God. It had been Ecgfrith himself who had begged Cuthbert to accept a bishopric;[67] and in Ecgfrith, as in his contemporary, Æthelbald of Mercia, one detects precisely that confusion of motive towards the Church that characterized the Merovingians. They are none the less warrior-kings with traditional appetites because they are haunted by the power of holy men. And there is another side to it: large gifts to churches and monasteries are not easy to guarantee at the best of times and may have to be revoked.

These contradictions are most plainly shown in the career of Bishop Wilfrid, as depicted by his biographer, Æddi. There is a Celtic strain in Wilfrid, less strong than in Cuthbert and Guthlac, rather overlaid by tastes and habits acquired among Merovingian and Roman clergy, but there, all the same. If Colgrave is right, one of Æddi's aims was to show how Wilfrid, sometimes through miracles, defended the integrity of the Church against 'the efforts of the Northumbrian kings to reduce it to subservience'.[68] This will be true only if we accept that the Church in Northumbria was not already and necessarily subservient. Even if Æddi did not, I find it easier to see Wilfrid's efforts as directed against kings who were outraged at what seemed to them new or unreasonable demands by the Church. The villain is King Ecgfrith, and Æddi sketches his relations with Wilfrid so boldly that one can scarcely believe that the Life was ever meant for royal eyes. The paucity of its manuscripts is

---

[65] *Two Lives of Saint Cuthbert*, ed. B. Colgrave (1940), pp. 102 ff.
[66] Ibid., p. 123.
[67] Ibid., p. 111.
[68] 'Earliest saints' lives', p. 56.

what one would have expected. From the beginning, Wilfrid's
career is bound up with kings and queens. His earliest patron
was Eanfled, Oswiu's queen,[69] who sent him to Lindisfarne and
later to Rome, by way of King Eorconberht of Kent, who much
admired his piety. On his return, and with the backing of King
Cenwalh of Wessex, he is warmly received by Alhfrith, Oswiu's
son. Alhfrith prostrates himself before Wilfrid, endows him
with lands and with Ripon for a monastery,[70] and they become
friends. 'Behold, brethren, see and wonder at the great benefit
God bestows upon the king, who "found a goodly pearl and
straightway bought it".' Alhfrith wishes Wilfrid to become a
priest and his inseparable companion. His wealth increases, in
Mercia as well as Northumbria. He is consecrated bishop in
Francia, only to find on his return that Chad has his see. This is
the first occasion of trouble. But there is another; for it seems
that it was on Wilfrid's advice that Æthelthryth, Ecgfrith's first
queen, took the veil; and this was never forgiven.[71] Æddi devotes
two chapters[72] to the contrasting fortunes of the first part of
Ecgfrith's reign, while he was 'obedient' to Wilfrid, and the
second, when he was not. It is a fact that Ecgfrith's prosperity *did*
coincide with Wilfrid's friendship and his decline with Wilfrid's
enmity. Above all the pro-Wilfrid Ecgfrith is prosperous in
battle. Æddi, and presumably Wilfrid himself, had no difficulty
in seeing a king's acquisitive warfare as God's warfare: 'trusting
in God like Judas Maccabeus, [Ecgfrith] attacked with his little
band of God's people an enemy host (the bestial Picts) which
was vast. . . . He slew an enormous number of the people, filling
two rivers with corpses . . . the tribes were reduced to slavery.'
The king, 'strong like David in crushing his enemies yet lowly in
the sight of God, breaking the necks of the tumultuous tribes
and their warlike kings', next turned on the wicked Wulfhere of
Mercia, so that 'countless numbers [of Mercians] were slain, the
king was put to flight and his kingdom laid under tribute'. In
fact, Ecgfrith was behaving much as Penda had behaved. The

[69] *The Life of Bishop Wilfrid by Eddius Stephanus*, ed. B. Colgrave (1927),
pp. 7, 9.
[70] Ibid., p. 17.
[71] Bede, *Hist. Eccl.* iv. 19. Cf. *Liber Eliensis*, ed. E. O. Blake (1962), i. 10.
[72] Chs. 19 and 20 (pp. 40–2).

difference was that the Church found it possible to support Ecgfrith in one of the most important and traditional occupations of barbarian kingship. This was no mere time-serving. It was not the simple adaptation of Christianity to the secular outlook of kings who meant anyway to go on campaigning in good pagan fashion, for the Church had long since decided that it was militant. When English churchmen began, as they may well now have done, to use what are called *comitatus*-terms to translate into the vernacular Latin words descriptive of God or Christ, they were not belatedly surrendering to a militancy they had failed to overcome.[73] The words employed, however, mattered less than the situations in which the Bible depicted kingship, whether of God or man. God's followers were a chosen people, not a *comitatus*, and Christ, though a king with a genealogy, was not a warrior. The warfare he required, and the obedience and loyalty this entailed, were in the first place spiritual. None the less, the two kinds of warfare had enough in common to explain why Æddi represented Wilfrid as the active supporter of the warrior Ecgfrith, and why Wilfrid himself probably was so.

Let me return to the text of Æddi. Having enriched Wilfrid, Ecgfrith regrets what he has given away, and, egged on by his second queen, Iurminburg, decides to take it back.[74] His instrument, according to Æddi, is Archbishop Theodore, though in fact Theodore had other reasons for dividing Wilfrid's huge diocese. There follows Wilfrid's appeal to Rome and Ecgfrith's refusal to accept the papal judgement. One is struck by the intensity of the king's resentment, which pursues Wilfrid on his retreat into Mercia and Wessex. What is more, Ecgfrith's successor, Aldfrith, inherits the vendetta. Further papal letters have no effect on him, though they prove slightly more efficacious in Mercia; and Aldfrith's successor, Eadwulf, is equally obdurate. It is only under *his* successor, Osred, that peace is finally made between king and bishop, with the help of suitable revelations. What more natural, then, than that Wilfrid should have left

[73] See the interesting observations of Green, *Carolingian Lord*, pp. 26, 161, 290, 303, 316, 400, 501.
[74] *Vita Wilf.*, p. 48.

money to his monks 'to purchase the friendship of kings and bishops'?[75] Motives apart, this complex story was not the invention of Æddi; its outlines are confirmed by other sources. And so we are left to explain how a seventh-century king first welcomes a holy man for his piety alone, then enriches him and makes him powerful, and finally decides to strip him of everything, even when threatened with papal excommunication. I do not discount the king's animosity about Queen Æthelthryth's taking the veil, common as it was for queens to do this, or the hostility of Queen Iurminburg; but the rift was also about property. One is back with the cry of King Chilperic in Gregory of Tours' *History*: 'look how the *fiscus* is impoverished and how all our wealth is in the hands of churches; only bishops reign nowadays and our honour is dead.'[76] 'Periet honor noster.' *Honor* is a difficult word,[77] but clearly it signifies the heart of royal authority. It is what goes when a king has been over-generous with gifts from his landed possessions. And this is the situation in which King Ecgfrith found himself. Wilfrid's endowments had been big, even by continental standards; big enough to deprive the king not only of wealth but also of influence. The king's reaction is not, then, surprising. What is surprising is that he should have parted with so much in the first place. It tells us something important about English kings of the first century after the conversion. It is a measure of the significance they attached to the support and prayers of the new holy men, and especially those of Celtic background. Even Queen Iurminburg, who hated Wilfrid, took her chance to steal a reliquary belonging to him; and it did her no good.[78] Wilfrid's wealth was unusual, though it was used to found and endow regular monasteries and not the bogus establishments deplored by Bede in a famous letter.[79] We have reached a time when the collective weight of such gifts throughout England must have been heavy indeed. It is illustrated by surviving charters which, comparatively few as they are, are numerous enough to show what

[75] Ibid., p. 137.
[76] *Hist. Lib.* vi. 46.
[77] Niermeyer, *Lexicon Minus*, lists 26 meanings for *honor*. See P. W. A. Immink, 'Honour, heerlijkheid en koningsgesag', *Tijdschr. v. Geschiedenis*, lxxiv (1961), pp. 285–308, and F. Lot, *Recueil des trav. hist.*, i, p. 361.
[78] *Vita Wilf.*, p. 78.
[79] *Epist. ad Ecgbertum episcopum*, ed. Plummer, i, pp. 414–15.

must have been happening more generally. Their proems are
doubtless the work of monastic beneficiaries, yet at the same time
they express something that was in the minds of the benefactors.
They agree about the God-given authority of kings, on the duty
of kings to protect and increase church property, and on the
fearsome consequences of any departure from this duty. The
common forms of the words they employ are not yet hackneyed
enough to be meaningless. Take, for example, the confirmation
and grant of Frithuwold, sub-king of Surrey under Wulfhere
of Mercia, to the monastery of Chertsey:[80] 'how often so ever we
devote anything to the members of Christ as an act of piety, we
trust to benefit our soul, because we render to him his own property, and do not bestow ours . . . I not only give the land but
confirm and deliver myself and my only son in obedience to
Abbot Eorconwold.' What Frithuwold gets in return is inter-
cession for the relief of his soul. The formula is common enough.
Nothelm, king of the South Saxons, grants his sister land for a
monastery at Lidsey and elsewhere 'because it will benefit me in
the future'.[81] The church is to be devoted to 'the divine praises
and honouring of the saints'. A note of insecurity sounds in the
grant by Offa, king of the East Saxons, of land at Hemel Hemp-
stead to the bishop of London: 'although the words of priests and
the decrees of royal ordinances remain in unshaken stability for
ever, yet because commonly the storms and whirlwinds of secular
concerns beat also at the gates of the Church. . . .'[82] Finally,
there is the Latin privilege granted to the churches and monasteries of Kent by Wihtred at Bapchild.[83] It is, he says, 'a fearful
thing for men to rob the living God' by seizing anything of his

[80] I cite the translation of D. Whitelock, *English Historical Documents*,
c. 500–1042 (1955), p. 440. Text in Kemble, *Codex Diplomaticus*, no. 987, and
Birch, *Cartularium Saxonicum*, no. 34. Cf. P. H. Sawyer, *Anglo-Saxon Charters*
(1968), no. 1165.
[81] Whitelock, p. 446; Kemble, no. 995; Birch, no. 78; Sawyer, no. 45.
[82] Whitelock, p. 449; Oxford, Bodley MS. James 23; Sawyer, no. 1784.
[83] Haddan and Stubbs, iii, pp. 238 ff. To Kentish documentation, landbooks
and the like, reaching back to this period, the anonymous author (of St.
Augustine's, Canterbury?) of the vernacular tenth-century text of hagio-
graphical material edited by F. Liebermann, *Die Heiligen Englands* (1889),
was presumably indebted. It is an important witness to continuing local interest
in the claims to sanctity of members of the royal Kentish dynasty and to its
connections with other royal dynasties, including the Franks. I am indebted to
Dr. W. A. Pantin for reminding me of this text.

worldly substance . . . 'neque de hac re aliquid pertineat ad regis saecularis imperium'. The Church has been busy with Wihtred, as his laws also betray. We can imagine that the proem to a charter might not interest a king so long as it was generally in tune with his views of his own authority; but a collection of laws must stand closer to him. So Wihtred, like his West Saxon contemporary, Ine, whose laws owe much to Kent,[84] legislates with the Church in the forefront of his mind. His aim is to protect it: it shall not be taxed, and in return the king shall be prayed for and honoured freely and without compulsion[85] (a strange phrase); its *mundbyrd* shall be fifty shillings, like the king's own. A similar equality is implied in the laws of Ine, with reference to breaking into royal and episcopal burhs.[86] Moreover, Ine is king 'by the grace of God',[87] and he legislates in council with his lay and clerical notables. The occasions of these law-makings or writings, if we can trust the prologues, puts one in mind of the Toledo councils. English thinking about kingship and law, direct or implied, is primitive indeed by the side of the Spanish pronouncements; but, like them, it owes whatever is new to the Church. So far as England is concerned, there is a sharp difference between the earliest Kentish legislation and what we find at the close of the seventh century. Between Æthelberht and Wihtred stand not only churchmen of the kind we have been considering but also Archbishop Theodore and his friends. That is to say, the influx of ideas and practices from the continent, both from Francia[88] and Rome. Gregory the Great, as we have seen, liked to lecture kings on their duties. After all, they were converts, or not far removed from predecessors who were. The seventh-century popes address kings who are rather more sophisticated. They need careful reminders, studied rebukes, and plenty of praise. One may instance Pope Vitalian's letter of 667 to King Oswiu on the subject of a new archbishop

---

[84] See Richardson and Sayles, *Law and Legislation*, pp. 13 ff. It is, however, uncertain whether Ine borrowed from Wihtred or the other way about.

[85] F. L. Attenborough, *The Laws of the Earliest English Kings* (1922), pp. 24 ff.; Liebermann, *Gesetze*, i, pp. 12 ff.

[86] Attenborough, p. 50, cl. 45; Liebermann, i, p. 108.

[87] Attenborough, prol., p. 36; Liebermann, i, p. 88.

[88] For Frankish influence in the seventh century, especially in Kent, see Stenton, *Anglo-Saxon England*, pp. 60-1.

of Canterbury.[89] It starts with a long paragraph of congratulation
and exhortation: 'happy the people', writes the pope, 'who have
as king a man so very wise and God-fearing', who spends days and
nights considering how to bring his people to the Catholic faith.
He cites the relevant passages of scripture. The king will now in
all things follow the 'piam regulam . . . principis apostolorum'.
This is reinforced by a present of relics of the Roman martyrs,
both for Oswiu and for his queen, and notably relics of St. Peter
and St. Paul. 'Festinet igitur quaesumus, vestra celsitudo, ut op-
tamus, totam suam insulam Deo Christo dicare.'[90] Rome may
favour small dioceses for England, but certainly it also favours
larger kingdoms. It was a helpful doctrine for kings. Plainly we
are already deep in the Petrine cult. The complex history of its
papal development need not delay us now; it has been much
studied;[91] but it needs to be said that its full flowering is post-
Gregorian. It is from the seventh century that successive popes
find their identification with St. Peter most useful in dealing with
Germanic kings. It recurs repeatedly in papal correspondence. In
adapting Christianity to barbarian needs, the popes found two
themes specially attractive to kings: the first was the theme of
warfare for Christ, and the second was that of obedience to St.
Peter.[92] In a world of holy men and relics, all efficacious for kings
who knew how to make use of them, none was more efficacious
than St. Peter. The letter of Pope Vitalian is a case in point. For
England there is further evidence in the conflict over St. Wilfrid.
Pope Agatho backs his decision on the restoration of Wilfrid to
his see with threats of excommunication, by the authority of St.
Peter, against all who disobey him, 'even a king';[93] and the threat

[89] Haddan and Stubbs, iii, pp. 110–12.
[90] This phrase illustrates what is easily overlooked: that the popes and
missionaries of the period saw the practical aim of their work as the conversion of all heathen, and not simply those near at hand or related by blood.
See W. H. Fritze, 'Universalis gentium confessio', Frühmittelalterliche Studien,
iii (1969), pp. 78–130.
[91] e.g. by W. Ullmann, The Growth of Papal Government in the Middle Ages
(2nd ed., 1962), and elsewhere; M. Maccarrone, 'La dottrina del primato papale
dal IV all'VIII secolo nelle relazioni con le Chiese occidentali', Settimane di
Studio, vii. 2 (1960); and, for dedications, by W. Levison, England and the Continent in the Eighth Century (1946), appendix v.
[92] See the comment of R. Buchner, Settimane di Studio, xiv, p. 508.
[93] Vita Wilf., ed. Colgrave, p. 67.

is reinforced, some years later, in a letter from Pope John to Kings Æthelred and Aldfrith: 'so remember, dear sons, what the blessed Agatho . . . ordained by apostolic authority about this matter. For whoever he be, of whatever rank, who despises us with bold temerity, shall not go unpunished.'[94] Such language has some effect, in the end. It is a term of reference in the making of the seventh-century idea of kingship, whether English or continental.

We can never know whether Roman ideas of kingship were conveyed to the English kings by Archbishop Theodore. The canons of his councils are concerned with other matters. But his Penitential suggests a man who would do much to placate kings as he found them. He was a co-operator, not a rebuker. His penitential *dicta*, if strictly applied, would have affected daily life in a way that kings could not have ignored; for instance, on the subject of manslaughter.[95] Yet we find these *dicta*, also: if treasure is seized from a conquered enemy, a third shall be given to the Church or to the poor, and penance shall be done for only forty days 'because it was the king's command';[96] 'if a king holds the territory of another king, he may give it [sc. to the Church] for [the good of] his soul';[97] a man entering religion who holds gifts in specie from a king should return them to the king.[98] Theodore does not repeat the recommendation of the Irish Cummean, whose Penitential he probably used, that 'we ought to offer the sacraments on behalf of good kings, never on behalf of evil kings'.[99] He takes kings as he finds them, in a very un-Irish way.[100] But it was not an un-Roman way.

Lastly, protruding into the scene of seventh-century kingship stands the barrow of Sutton Hoo. Ten years ago I advanced some

[94] Ibid., pp. 119–21.
[95] Haddan and Stubbs, iii, p. 180 (*De occisione hominum*); J. T. McNeill and H. M. Gamer, *Medieval Handbooks of Penance* (repr., New York, 1965), p. 187.
[96] Haddan and Stubbs, iii, p. 182 (*De multis vel diversis malis et quae non nocent necessaria*, 2); McNeill and Gamer, p. 190.
[97] Haddan and Stubbs, iii, p. 202 (*De diversis questionibus*, 7); McNeill and Gamer, p. 212.
[98] Ibid., cl. 8.
[99] Ibid., p. 112.
[100] It is hard to accept Professor Deanesly's view (*The Pre-Conquest Church in England*, p. 106) that Vitalian appointed him as a man broad enough to cope sympathetically with the Celtic north.

reasons why I hesitated to accept Sutton Hoo as specifically royal.[101] I still feel a little of that in me that caused Sancho Panza to beg Don Quixote not to take the barber's basin for Mambrino's helmet. But I was careful not to suggest that Sutton Hoo could not be royal. Assuming now that it is, let us see what it has to say of kingship. If the great barrow had contained a royal burial it would, later than the mid-seventh century, present very serious problems of interpretation. But apparently it did not; and its date may be before the mid-century. There is no objection to the by now traditional solution of thinking of it as a kind of memorial to a dead king, or even to a king who had resigned his power; indeed, I rather prefer the latter. It would then be a kind of burial; the burial of a man's military career, a gesture such as Guthlac might have made. There is no objection so long as this, too, is allowed to be a provisional solution. A king, presumably East Anglian, is commemorated by the burying in a ship of his war-gear and costly objects associated with him, some of it old and much of it magnificent. No one would have suspected that an out-of-the-way dynasty such as this could command such treasure. If we had any contemporary English royal grave to compare it with, we might be less surprised. However, these particular memorial-goods are in a fundamental sense what we should expect: they are as barbaric as the hall of Heorot. They are a manifestation of Germanic wealth and power, and seem to look back in a political sense though forward in an artistic. So we accept the whole affair as splendidly old-fashioned, quite out of tune with what we can guess about the burial of Æthelberht at Canterbury or Edwin at York. Yet there is no reason why Æthelberht or Edwin should have been buried with a puritanical simplicity designed to contrast with their pagan ancestors' splendid burials. Oswald was to lie in his tomb at Bardney under his standard and his gold and purple banner, as befitted a *regia persona*,[102] and a young Merovingian prince was buried in Cologne Cathedral in the mid-sixth century complete with

---

[101] 'The graves of kings: an historical note on some archaeological evidence', *Studi medievali*, 3rd series, I. i (1960), pp. 177–94. The archaelogy is brilliantly summarized by R. L. S. Bruce-Mitford in *The Sutton Hoo ship burial: a handbook* (2nd ed., 1968), pending the publication of the British Museum's definitive study in four volumes.

[102] Bede, *Hist. Eccl.* iii. 11.

helmet, shield, weapons, and a little wooden stave.[103] Sutton Hoo
need not be so backward-looking after all. There is nothing that
we can call ritually pagan or Christian about it, and no reason
why there should be, if it is not a burial. If among the memorial-
goods there are any insignia of royalty, not one of them need have
offended a Christian missionary or even a well-established bishop.
Whetstone and standard, helmet and weapons and lyre, would
not have struck him as un-Christian. Who dearer to Christians
than the harpist David? They could well be the tools of any
Christian king who cheerfully went to war with his neighbours, in
the way that Bede so often describes. If the two silver spoons, inscribed 'Saulos' and 'Paulos',[104] and the silver bowls, were personal
to the king I am supposing to have been commemorated, they
would perhaps make him a Christian; but they would not make
Sutton Hoo Christian. In brief, though witnessing to intense feeling, the occasion has nothing formally religious about it, in the
sense that we are dealing with any known or accepted part of religious ritual. We are not to imagine Sutton Hoo as an unexpected
field-day for the pagans, with a bishop wringing his hands in the
background. But it belongs to a time when the king in question
was as likely to be a Christian as a pagan; and it is a warning to
take seriously the transitional nature of seventh-century Christianity, as also of kingship. The Church compromises, partly
because its teaching permits it, partly because it has to. The converted kings accept with caution a new God who can be useful to
them in a variety of ways. Sutton Hoo is not in any ceremonial
sense a mixture of Christian and pagan. But it belongs to precisely
the time when the religion of kings contained elements of both;
and if of kings, then also of those who commemorated them.
In so far as Sutton Hoo connotes any religious background at
all, it confirms the idea that we have of seventh-century kingship.

[103] Cf. J. Werner, *Antiquity*, xxxviii, pp. 206–11.
[104] R. E. Kaske, 'The silver spoons of Sutton Hoo', *Speculum*, xlii (1967),
pp. 670–2, thinks that both spoons may read 'Paulos' and be the work of
different craftsmen. If so, they may, as Dr. Bruce-Mitford points out to me,
be more in the nature of souvenirs from a workshop producing spoons than a
specific conversion pair. But this is uncertain: they may still have been
regarded as a pair. Another instance of the 'co-existence' of paganism and
Christianity is the series of scenes on the Franks Casket, on which see H. R.
Ellis Davidson, 'The Smith and the Goddess', *Frühmittelalterliche Studien*, iii
(1969), pp. 216–26.

IV

BEDE

BEDE's mind was full of kings; so, too, his writings. To understand why and in what sense this was so, we need to know not only all that can be known of the political circumstances of his time but also what he read. Probably we over-estimate the extent of his knowledge of public affairs; certainly, we underestimate the extent to which his book-knowledge penetrated and shaped his judgement of those affairs. We cannot yet always be sure when Bede himself is speaking directly and not paraphrasing, alluding to, or being unconsciously influenced by an earlier writer. Nor can we always know which writer. Laistner's well-known and still useful list[1] of books used by Bede tells only part of the story. For my present purposes, what matters is that he was saturated in certain identifiable writings that contain forceful and compelling outlooks on kingship. This is why we cannot proceed to his own *History* until we have looked a little at this background of books.

The influence of Eusebius is obvious;[2] his *Ecclesiastical History* was known to Bede in the Latin translation of Rufinus, and its last book was one of his models for the picture of a ruler victorious through conversion. The final chapter of Eusebius' *History*, with its account of the growing insanity of the godless Licinius and the victorious progress of Constantine, supported by the Christian God in material as well as other ways, at once calls to mind comparable occasions in the narratives of several barbarian historians, Bede included. Moreover, the direct influence of Eusebius on Bede was reinforced by Bede's reading of another Eusebian enthusiast, Gildas. Less obvious is the influence of

---

[1] 'The library of the venerable Bede', repr. in *The Intellectual Heritage of the Early Middle Ages* (New York, 1957), pp. 145–9.

[2] See J. Campbell, 'Bede', in *Latin Historians*, ed. T. A. Dorey, esp. pp. 162–3; also D. S. Wallace-Hadrill, *Eusebius of Caesarea* (1960), pp. 155–89.

Augustine; less obvious and harder to assess, since Augustine's views on earthly rule were neither neatly collected nor easy to grasp. Impressed by such of Augustine's theological and exegetical work as he knew, Bede seems not to have felt the impact of the *De Civitate Dei*, which he certainly read, in a political way. He may have assimilated something of the outlook of the famous chapter 24 of Book 5, with its picture of imperial *felicitas* based on Christian *iustitia* and personal humility, but he certainly attached a higher value than Augustine did to the prosperity and victory that were the material consequences of good rule. It is early days to speak of Bede's debt to Augustine; so also of the influence on him of Isidore. The *Etymologiae* and perhaps the *Sententiae*[3] were available to him, and I have the impression that Isidore's definitions of kingship may lie behind more than one of Bede's judgements on the kings of whom he wrote. Yet neither Isidore nor Augustine affected his idea of earthly rule as it was affected by Gregory the Great's exalted sense of the divine nature of kingship. The extent of the debt here is one aspect only of a greater question that is 'involved and complex'.[4] It must be enough to draw attention to the effect on Bede of the *Liber Regulae Pastoralis*; indeed, it is one of the principal distinctions between Bede and Gregory of Tours as historians that the first used the *Pastoral Care* and the second did not.[5] The intention of the pope's book had been to investigate the nature of episcopal rule; but his words were susceptible of wider application. What he wrote of the rule of bishops could be more generally understood, and even applied to kings. This is important: those who did most to reinterpret kingship were to be monks, and it is a monastic view of authority, whether of bishop or abbot, that harmonizes most comfortably with monarchical power. Another instance of the same kind of interchange is provided by the Carolingian abbot Smaragdus, who found that whole sections of his work called the *Via Regia* could be incorporated into a

---

[3] Compare their descriptions of David.

[4] Dom P. Meyvaert, 'Bede and Gregory the Great', *Jarrow Lecture* (1964), p. 13.

[5] I have already drawn attention to this in my 'Gregory of Tours and Bede: their views on the personal qualities of kings', *Frühmittelalterliche Studien*, ii (1968), which is in part a preliminary sketch for this chapter.

book of a different kind, the *Diadema Monachorum*.[6] Two recommendations in Gregory's book could be applied to secular rulers with some force. The first was that the moral quality of the ruler was what counted; and the second was that rule of any kind was a professional occupation, calling for special aptitudes, training, and constant self-examination. No page of the *Pastoral Care* lacks these two lessons. They were not lost on Bede, nor on a succession of other Englishmen, King Alfred included. For Bede, then, secular rule had a moral basis, a necessary equipment, and clearly defined Christian objectives; and this was bound to affect his approach to the interpretation of what kings had actually done, as well as what they ought to be doing. Their aims could no longer be confined to the comparative simplicities of fighting the right enemies and endowing the right churches. He seems to want his kings to rule their subjects in the spirit in which Pope Gregory meant his bishops to rule their flocks. They must show a certain professionalism or go under. Neither Bede nor Gregory had achieved a full-fledged doctrine of kingship, but they were feeling their way towards one.

Yet two more books contributed to Bede's ideas of rule. One of them was Gildas's *De Excidio*. The debt is not confined to those passages of Romano-British history which he cites *in extenso*; perhaps they are the smaller part of it. Gildas was clear that a nation had a destiny under God,[7] that its prosperity bore a direct relationship to its salvation, and its declension to sin. Within this context its rulers bore responsibility for success or failure. They could be of well-nigh heroic stature, whether for good or evil, and Gildas lost no opportunity of saying so. He was as frank about his contemporaries as was Gregory of Tours; so much so, that it is impossible to believe that either meant his work to fall into the hands of the kings he castigated. Bede took no such risks. Gildas's picture of the British tyrants is extraordinary: they

---

[6] Smaragdus' writings will be found in *Pat. Lat.* cii. See the important commentary by Anton, *Fürstenspiegel*, ch. 3. It may be worth noting that the Irish had several king-abbots, all, as my pupil, Mr. Alfred P. Smyth, kindly informs me, of Munster, with their seat at Cashel. One such, Feidlimid mac Crimthainn, who died in 847, is briefly discussed by D. A. Binchy, *Celtic and Anglo-Saxon Kingship*, p. 42.

[7] So R. W. Hanning, *The Vision of History in Early Britain* (New York, 1966), who draws attention to Bede's use of Eusebius and Gildas in ch. 3.

were murderers, adulterers, perjurors, oppressors, liars; their wars were civil wars, unjust wars; their forfeitures hugely exceeded their almsgiving; they reduced themselves to the level of animals —lions, leopards, bears, and dragons—much in the manner of Fredegar's Merovingians. But behind the tirade lurk traces of Christian kings face to face with problems familiar to kings elsewhere and not peculiar to sixth-century Britain: they were only what Stevens calls 'rough men'.[8] The tyrant Maglocunus of Anglesey, who took monastic vows and then had second thoughts; or Cuneglas, who put away his wife in favour of her sister, a nun; or Aurelius Caninus, who clearly believed that his religious merit, whatever it was, would excuse him his crimes; these and others were not rude barbarians, let alone wild beasts. Yet so Gildas portrays them. Part at least of his inspiration lay in the Bible, with which he was very familiar. It really begs the question to regret that he gave so little space to the politics of his own day and so much to biblical exemplars.[9] The kings of the Bible and those of sixth-century Britain were inextricably woven in his mind and in his narrative.[10] Most notably, he is prepared to draw direct parallels between biblical and present-day kings; the same kind of fate awaits any *rex iniquus*, whatever his period. One may instance his judgement on Ahab;[11] or, in another context, 'hoc in tyrannis nostri temporis perspicue deprehenditur';[12] or again, referring to priests, we want, he says, more brave priests, like Samuel, 'absque adulatione regem'.[13] He saw himself in the same line of business. Hezekiah, on the other hand, was a *rex*

[8] 'Gildas Sapiens', *Engl. Hist. Rev.* lvi (1941), p. 366. For Gildas's historical background see I. LL. Foster, 'The emergence of Wales' in *Prehistoric and Early Wales* (1965). J. N. L. Myres, 'Pelagius and the end of Roman rule in Britain', *Journ. Roman Studies*, l (1960) should also be consulted.

[9] As, for example, did F. Lot, *Recueil*, i, p. 784.

[10] I am not persuaded by the arguments of P. Grosjean, 'Notes d'hagiographie celtique', *Anal. Boll.* lxxv (1957), esp. p. 203, that only part of the *De Excid.* was known to Bede and that in any case we must see a 'forger' at work on the text. F. Kerlouégan, 'Le latin du De Excidio Britanniae de Gildas', in *Christianity in Britain, 300–700* (1968), ed. M. W. Barley and R. P. C. Hanson, believes in the linguistic unity of the work. In his admirable *Christianity in Early Britain* (1912) Hugh Williams grasped the significance of Gildas's biblical expertise (p. 449).

[11] *MGH Auct. Ant.* XIII, ed. Mommsen, p. 50.

[12] Ibid., p. 60.

[13] Ibid., p. 66.

pius, for whom God smote 185,000 Assyrian warriors in their tents.[14] I am not claiming anything original for Gildas's exegesis; but it is still the case that he relates the fortunes of the Israelites and especially of their kings in a startlingly direct manner to those of his British contemporaries. Bede knew his Gildas; and he knew his Bible even better.

Bede's biblical commentaries bristle with technical problems that I am incompetent to pursue. One of them is the extent of his indebtedness to earlier patristic commentaries. But this at least we can say: that whatever the source of his words, he makes them his own and they express his personal judgement. We may look briefly, since it is most relevant here, at his commentary on 1 Samuel, written about the year 716. Like most of his commentaries, it is predominantly allegorical; it was not his concern to connect biblical events with present issues in the manner of Gildas. But he covers dangerous ground; kings are kings, whenever they live; and the first king of many on whom Bede expressed a considered opinion was King Saul. The Israelites wanted a king, like other people; and they wanted him for military reasons, from which his rule would be inseparable.[15] Samuel prophesied what sort of king they would get: he would not be a 'moderatus et justus imperator', as Christ was to be, not a *bonus rex* but a *rector improbus*, a *rex impius*, who would oppress them.[16] The characteristics of a good king would be *prudentia, fortitudo, iustitia*, and *temperantia*. As Bede looked at Saul, his point of reference was Christ as king, 'qui de omnium regum qui solus salvavit de universis malis rex constituitur'.[17] Samuel said that king and people would be destroyed if they ceased to fear God, and Bede goes so far as to comment that though Samuel was speaking of the Israelites, still 'sub eiusdem regis figura, variantia totius eorum regni tempora comprehendit'.[18] Kings who do not fear God bring down their kingdoms with them; bad weather and poor harvests are a sign of this.[19]

[14] *MGH Auct. Ant.* XIII, ed. Mommsen, p. 67.
[15] The point is made by J. Funkenstein, 'Unction of the ruler', in *Adel und Kirche* (Tellenbach Festschrift, Freiburg, 1968), pp. 8–11.
[16] Ed. D. Hurst, *Corpus Christianorum*, cxix, pt. ii, 2 (Turnholt, 1962), p. 72.
[17] Ibid., p. 90.
[18] Ibid., p. 98.
[19] Ibid., p. 99.

Saul had begun well, living humbly and privately, 'nec regio habitu indui ceteraque regni insignia sumere curavit'; nor did he surround himself with warriors.[20] He came to grief through disobedience and pride, and so lost his kingdom. In his place David, the prefiguration of Christ, was anointed king. Yet there was something sacred about the old king. Despite Samuel's own intention in passing on his charismatic power to Saul by unction, the Israelites felt Saul to be something like a god-king, in whom dwelt special power not because of unction but because he was king.[21] David regretted cutting off the fringe of the robe of his anointed *dominus*[22] and refused to kill the sleeping king 'qui Iudaici populi regnum specialiter ei a domino datum est et oleo sancto consecratum'.[23] Instead, he took Saul's spear: 'hasta vel ipsam regni potentiam vel arma virtutum spiritalium quibus regnum iuvare poterat insinuat'.[24] Achish, to whom David flees, says to him, 'therefore will I make thee keeper of mine head for ever', on which Bede comments: 'Patet iuxta litteram quia pro-mittente David auxilium regi, promittit et ipse custodem capitis sui sive in belli certamine seu post victoriam se eum esse facturum.'[25] Perhaps Bede was thinking of other times, nearer home; perhaps also when he read that, when Saul and his armour-bearer died together, the Philistines took his head, hung up his body, and put his armour in the temple of Astaroth; and finally his men recovered the body, burnt it, and buried the bones.[26] Bede draws only the most discreet and general parallels with modern times, and yet one feels throughout his commentary that he can see Saul in modern terms. The very words of the text are laden with special meaning for him: *imperium, lex, ius, fidelis, amicus, inimicus, ultio, sermo regis, convivium regis, hasta, gens,* and above all *rex* itself. Always the kingship of Christ, the *rex regum*, is present to him, from the first appearance of a king of Israel. Saul started well in his sacrosanct office and knew his business, but failed in obedience. The result of his failure was

[20] Ibid., p. 102.
[21] Cf. Funkenstein, 'Unction', p. 8.
[22] Ed. Hurst, p. 226.
[23] Ibid., p. 244.
[24] Ibid., p. 245.
[25] Ibid., p. 253.
[26] Ibid., pp. 270-1.

death for him and, for his people, military defeat and political humiliation. One of Bede's rare biblical citations in the *Ecclesiastical History* refers to Saul. Admiringly, he compares the warrior Æthelfrith of Northumbria[27] to Saul in these words: 'cui merito poterat illud quod benedicens filium patriarcha in personam Saulis dicebat aptari: Benjamin lupus rapax, mane comedet praedam et vespere dividit spolia.'[28]

It has seemed worth while to draw attention, if no more, to these strands in Bede's thinking. Without Eusebius, Gregory, Isidore, Gildas, and the Bible with its commentators, it is impossible to believe that he could have constructed his picture of modern kings quite in the way he did. The kingship that mattered to him was a historical institution, originating in Israel, not in the forests of Germany. For this reason, the transition from the commentary on 1 Samuel to the *Ecclesiastical History* is an easy one: they have more in common than at first strikes the eye. Bede's reading had taught him that peoples—and the *Ecclesiastical History* is about a people—were brought to Christianity, and sustained in it to their prosperity or plunged from it into disaster, by kings. Kings were the focal point of conversion; without them, the propagation of the new faith and the encouragement of its teachers were inconceivable. The unity of a people rested not in a common language nor in its occupation of a former Roman province but in its religion. No royal duty seemed more urgent than the eradication of religious disunity— that is to say, heresy. In so far as kings were successful in guiding their people towards Catholic orthodoxy, they and their people might win a present reward in the shape of victory and prosperity. This is why kings were central to Bede's historical narrative; and in this context, rather than in the political state of affairs in eighth-century England, Bede found the stimulus to write history. He does not say that anyone ordered him to write history, though he acknowledges that he was urged to it by Albinus of Canterbury. The initiative was his own.

We should pause to consider what he does say about Albinus. Albinus had incited him to write: 'ad quam me scribendam

---

[27] Not Æthelberht of Kent, as stated by Hanning, *Vision of History*, p. 84.
[28] *Hist. Eccl.* i. 34; Genesis 49:27.

iamdudum instigaveras.'[29] He had done this in part by furnishing much material; so much, that Bede felt that his principal debt was to Canterbury. And it went far beyond material concerning the affairs of Kent. We must reckon, then, with the possibility that Bede's history may have been affected by Canterbury's wish to bring history to the service of present needs. Canterbury was well served in what was written. It is a matter that could bear investigation.[30]

A further consideration is that Bede dedicates his history to the Northumbrian king, Ceolwulf; likely enough, from him, too, he had received encouragement. Other books of that age had been dedicated to kings: Isidore's *De Natura Rerum* was dedicated to the learned king Sisebut, and Fulgentius sent his anti-Arian treatise to king Thrasamund. Both books were known to Bede, but neither was a history. Bede's dedication reveals more: Ceolwulf had seen a first draft of the history, and was then sent a fair copy. The king was expected to make use of it; he and his subjects should profit from its lessons. At a guess, they were to regard it as one more Christian substitute for the historical matter of their traditional Germanic songs.[31] We have, then, this assurance about Bede's picture of kingship: it had proved acceptable to the author's king and thus had something of an official stamp.

No one supposes that Bede tells us all that he knew about kings; however hard it may have been to come by, his material was carefully selected. His picture of them, as indeed of the wider scene, is an artefact designed for a particular purpose and intended to leave a particular impression on readers and hearers. There are passages in his history where Bede can be shown, possibly to have suppressed information, certainly to have selected and presented it in a way that others could have disapproved of. I am not concerned with these, nor with their implications, but only to make the point that Bede takes the facts that

---

[29] The letter to Albinus is printed in Plummer's ed. on the unnumbered page following I, p. clxxviii.

[30] Miss Marion Gibbs shows one way in which this can be undertaken in an unpublished work which she was kind enough to allow me to read.

[31] The hymn in honour of Queen Æthelthryth inserted in *Hist. Eccl.* iv. 20 suggests a modest challenge to Virgil, though nothing is said of Germanic epic.

suit him and that are relevant to what could be called a narrative of national salvation. With this in mind, I turn to the problem not of what the early English kings actually did but of what Bede thought of what they did, and why. Of course, the distinction is not always clear-cut. Bede himself is evidence that some kings acted upon the Church's teaching about kingship. And Bede was read by kings. It was not long before the *Ecclesiastical History* was in other royal hands than those of Ceolwulf; in England, Offa had a copy,[32] and so did Alfred.

There were two categories of good king that arrested Bede's attention. The first can be called that of the warrior-convert, the second that of the saintly or monk-king or queen. They are naturally interwoven in his narrative, as chronology required. Taking the warrior-converts first, Æthelberht of Kent has priority. Bede insists that things went well for the king and his subjects after conversion, as the missionaries had promised: he reigned over his kingdom for fifty-six years *gloriosissime*.[33] He was not to Bede what Clovis had been to Gregory of Tours, the heroic figure of the conversion of the English at large; he is not *christianissimus*, there is nothing to suggest that the Church of Canterbury attempted to make him the object of a cult, and there is no evidence of a popular cult, either.[34] The fate of King Edwin of Northumbria was very different, and to him Bede devoted more attention. He, too, had been a pagan warrior and had received a promise of increase of power in return for conversion and as an earnest of the kingdom of heaven.[35] It is clear that he won back his kingdom while still a pagan and only undertook to accept Christianity if God gave him victory over his enemy, Cwichelm of Wessex: 'si vitam sibi et victoriam donaret pugnanti adversus regem'.[36] Bede's account, however,

[32] So we learn from a letter to Offa from Alcuin, reprinted from Lehmann's edition by Levison, *England and the Continent*, p. 245.

[33] *Hist. Eccl.* ii. 5.

[34] There is, however, some evidence of belated recognition by Canterbury of the potentialities of the Kentish royal family. See *Acta Sanctorum*, Oct., viii, pp. 100–3.

[35] *Hist. Eccl.* ii. 9.

[36] Ibid. His words recall those attributed to Clovis at Tolbiac by Gregory of Tours: 'tuae opis gloriam devotus efflagito, ut, si mihi victuriam super hos hostes indulseris et expertus fuero illam virtutem, quam de te populus tuo nomine dicatus probasse se praedicat, credam tibi et in nomine tuo baptizer' (*Hist. Lib.* ii. 30).

betrays the existence of already well-developed miracle-stories centred on Edwin's early career.[37] Whether they are really evidence of a secular cult in the sense of popular saga is open to question,[38] though in part they may be. The Church at least had been busy with Edwin in the century between his death and the writing of the *Ecclesiastical History*. Cautious though he was after victory to make good his word by accepting conversion, the king did reign gloriously thereafter, for six years. The peace of those years on which Bede dwells[39] looks to have nothing specifically Christian about it; it owed most to the *timor* and the *amor* that the king inspired. Yet, as we shall see, fear in the hearts of his enemies, internal and external, and love in the hearts of his faithful subjects were precisely the sentiments that the teachers of the Church insisted that a good king should inspire. They were the condition of material prosperity and national prestige. But what made the real difference was the manner of the king's death. He fell in a great battle at Hatfield, fighting Cadwallon and Penda for reasons which, whatever they were, were not religious. His enemies were ready enough to destroy his church-buildings, but their long and bitter feud with the Northumbrians was clearly dynastic in a general sense. Towards the end of his life, Penda was not ill-disposed towards Christianity. He cannot have fought his wars to eradicate it. Cadwallon, moreover, was a Christian. Yet there can be no doubt that the paganism of Penda was important to the Church, both on this occasion when he was subordinate to Cadwallon and later when he was not. His role in Church historiography was negative but vital, rather like that of Ebroin in Frankish tradition.[40] Not only were the kings whom he killed Christians but by falling to him, a pagan, they became candidates for martyrdom. This eventually is what happened to Edwin: 'martyrio coronatus vitae terminum

[37] P. Hunter Blair, 'Bede's Ecclesiastical History of the English Nation and its importance today', *Jarrow Lecture* (1959), discusses the significance of miracles to Bede; see also B. Colgrave, 'Bede's miracle stories', in *Bede, his Life, Times and Writings*, ed. A. Hamilton Thompson (1932).
[38] C. E. Wright, *The Cultivation of Saga in Anglo-Saxon England* (1939), believes that Bede's account is based 'on the mass of oral traditions current' though he concedes that it may owe 'something, perhaps much, to Bede's literary skill' (p. 91).
[39] *Hist. Eccl.* ii. 16.
[40] As Graus sees, *Volk, Herrscher und Heiliger*, p. 417, n. 689.

consummavit.'[14] There is no telling how soon the process began. What Bede knew was that at some time after the battle, the king's head was brought to York and placed in the portico of Pope Gregory in St. Peter's Church, which he himself had begun to build.[42] In another context, Bede adds that his body was buried at Whitby.[43] It had presumably been dismembered by Cadwallon or Penda in token of vengeance taken.[44] But Bede knew nothing of any cultus. For this we must turn to the anonymous Whitby Life of Gregory the Great, independent of Bede but contemporaneous. The Whitby writer describes the miraculous finding of Edwin's remains and reports that they were taken to Whitby: 'and now the holy bones are honourably buried in the Church of St. Peter . . . together with other of our kings, on the south side of the altar dedicated to St. Gregory, which is in the same church.'[45] He adds that 'the light of Christ shines from this King Edwin in the glory of his miracles in order that his merits may blaze forth more brightly'.[46] So it looks as if York got the head and Whitby the rest of the body, and that not long after the battle. Dr. Colgrave may have been right to suggest that the two royal princesses, Eanflaed and Ælfflaed, joint abbesses of Whitby, hoped that the remains of their relative would do for Whitby what King Oswald's relics were doing for the not far-distant house of Bardney.[47] In point of fact, the Whitby account of Edwin and Bede's of Oswald, to which I shall turn, are strangely alike, but that is no reason why one should have been modelled on the other. It seems extraordinary that Bede should not have known of the cult of Edwin at Whitby, or, if he knew it, should not have reported it—unless, of course, he disbelieved some part of the Whitby claim; for he does his best for Edwin. Nevertheless, it is from the Whitby writer, not from Bede, that we

[41] *Vita Oswaldi*, i. 2 (Symeon of Durham, i, Rolls Series, p. 341). See also *Acta Sanct.*, Oct., vi, pp. 108–19.
[42] *Hist. Eccl.* ii. 20.
[43] Ibid. iii. 24.
[44] So Plummer thought, ed., *Hist. Eccl.* ii. p. 116.
[45] Ed. B. Colgrave, *The Earliest Life of Gregory the Great* (Lawrence, 1968), p. 105. The 'kings' were: Oswiu and Edwin, apart from the royal abbesses 'and many other noble persons' according to Bede (*Hist. Eccl.* iii. 24).
[46] Ed. Colgrave, p. 101.
[47] Ibid., p. 43.

learn that the relics of the martyr-king worked miracles and were the object of a local cult. Edwin had achieved a distinction denied to the Merovingians, and presumably to any English king before his time. Bede, however, went as far as he could: the head at York was a genuine English royal relic, closely associated in its resting-place with the apostle of the English. He meant it to be understood that the king had gone some way towards acting on the advice given him by Pope Honorius in a letter that is included in the *Ecclesiastical History*: 'your conduct as king', the pope wrote, 'is based on the knowledge you have obtained of God', and he recommends the king to study the writings of Gregory the Great.[48] And yet, one feels, a more thorough-going submission to the Church would have been possible in Bede's eyes.

The consequences of such submission are brought out more clearly in Bede's account of two of Edwin's Northumbrian successors, Oswald and Oswine. Ordered prosperity, like Edwin's, plays less part in his account of these later careers, and the reader's attention is focused on the sense these kings had of acting as God's agents and on their personal saintliness. Oswald in particular is beloved of God, affable and generous,[49] pious and humble.[50] Piety and humility were the qualities that Bede's reading had taught him were most to be sought for in a king; they made kings more kingly. Oswald's piety, indeed, brought with it an increase in rule above what his predecessors had enjoyed,[51] but this made no difference to his personal humility, one aspect of which was generosity to the poor. Bede gives an instance of this. Kings should take a paternal interest in all their subjects, rich and poor, and not confine their affection to their warriors. What was more, Oswald's conquests had the effect of spreading Christianity; he could be represented as a missionary-king.[52] Between Bede's lines, and occasionally in them, one can glimpse a reign a good deal devoted to the traditional Germanic pursuits of war. Oswald's claim to rule outside Bernicia was

[48] *Hist. Eccl.* ii. 17.
[49] Ibid. iii. 6.
[50] Ibid. 2.
[51] Ibid. 6.
[52] Ibid. 3.

questionable; and it was not his legitimacy but the divine assistance he attracted that Bede emphasizes: he was *victoriosissimus* because he was *sanctissimus*.[53] We are not told why he fell out with Penda, who defeated and killed him at Maserfelth.[54] It seems likely that Oswald and other kings directly associated with Celtic missionaries would have imbibed something of Irish teaching on the moral duties of kings; but we are not concerned with what sort of a king Oswald really was, so much as with how Bede chose to represent him. The royal cult already developed in Bede's time would have engendered most of the material he needed for his picture. The centres of the cult were Bardney, Hexham, and Bamburgh, and the details of his story suggest that these, and not any spontaneous popular tales, were Bede's principal source.[55] Like Edwin, Oswald fell in battle to Penda, 'pro patria dimicans', as a Christian champion. He, too, was a martyr, though Bede does not use the word. The place where he fell was not at once marked or considered as a holy place; his head and arms were left for months exposed on the stakes to which Penda affixed them. The place had to be 'revealed'. What is more, when his remains were first buried they were not seen as holy relics, and the monks of Bardney were not at all anxious to receive the body of a former enemy. What made the difference was the action of his family. Osthryth caused her uncle's body to be brought to Bardney, where it lay with his gold and purple banner erect above his tomb.[56] Her success was more startling than was that of the rescuers of Edwin's remains. Oswiu rescued Oswald's severed hands and took them to Bamburgh,[57] where they lay unwithered in their reliquary; and his head he buried in the church at Lindisfarne.[58] Bede had no doubt that miracles were commonly performed at places associated with the king; his patronage was as powerful in death as in life.[59] In brief, Oswald

[53] *Hist. Eccl.* iii. 1, 2, 6, 7.
[54] Ibid. 9.
[55] Cf. Graus, op. cit., p. 418.
[56] *Hist. Eccl.* iii. 11.
[57] Ibid. 12.
[58] And is now alleged to lie in St. Cuthbert's coffin at Durham. Cf. *The Relics of Saint Cuthbert*, ed. C. F. Battiscombe (1956), esp. pp. 96–8. For the further history of these relics see Plummer, vol. ii, pp. 157–8, and Graus, op. cit., p. 419.
[59] See the story of how Oswald stooped down from heaven on the anniversary

owed his posthumous reputation to the church he had befriended
and for which he could be represented as having died in battle;
his cult was ecclesiastical, not popular, in origin;[60] and it was
localized. There is no evidence of any general outburst of affection for the memory of the dead king. His family, with the
assistance of the Church, put him in the way of becoming a royal
saint, a miracle-worker. Such is Bede's picture.

Two further kings were indebted to Penda for a like service.
Sigebert, *rex religiosus* of the East Angles and once a notable
warrior, was brought out from the monastery to which he had
retired, to fight Penda, and was killed, *virga* in hand.[61] It was to
his death, not to his life, that later generations attributed his
sanctity.[62] Similarly with his successor, Anna, father of a saintly
progeny, 'qui et ipse postea ab eodem pagano Merciorum duce,
a quo et prodecessores eius, occisus est'.[63] Both kings, slain by a
pagan, could be seen as martyrs.

When he comes to the Northumbrian Oswine, Bede again
emphasizes his possession of the moral qualities the Church held
proper to the office of king. Like Oswald he was a *rex humilis*.
The humility was of a special kind and is illustrated by the story
of the king's gift of a horse to Bishop Aidan, of his anger when
he heard that the horse had been given by the bishop to a
beggar, and of his eventual capitulation to the bishop. It was not
the king who gave the splendid beast to the beggar, it was the
bishop. The point of the story lies in the words attributed to the
king: 'never again will I speak of this matter, nor will I decide
what, or how much, of my money you shall give to God's sons';[64]
and in Aidan's reaction to them: 'numquam enim ante haec vidi
humilem regem; his people were not worthy of such a ruler,
and he must shortly die.' The gifts of a good king, then, will
be lavished as his bishop chooses, and not otherwise; he will

of his death to summon an oblate boy, stricken with plague, to join him in
bliss: a saintly king continues to interest himself in his people (*Hist. Eccl.*
iii. 12).

[60] There are indeed 'popular' traits in subsequent developments of the
cult.

[61] *Hist. Eccl.* iii. 18.
[62] *Acta Sanct.*, Oct., xii. pp. 892–904.
[63] *Hist. Eccl.* iii 18; *Acta Sanct.*, Oct., xii, p. 899.
[64] *Hist. Eccl.* iii. 14.

owe to his bishop neither more nor less than obedience. Royal humility is obedience to the Church. The political consequences could have been alarming.[65] But there was more to Oswine than one story could convey. His was a golden reign of *affluentia*.[66] His personal qualities—he was handsome, tall, affable, courteous, and open-handed—were kingly, both those he inherited and those he acquired; he attracted followers from far afield, though not enough to save him from his neighbour, King Oswiu, on whose orders he was assassinated. He did not fall in battle, nor was he killed by a pagan; but he qualified, in the end, for martyrdom. Curiously, the first step in the process was taken by Oswiu's wife, Eanfled, moved by remorse either for the assassination or for the act of treachery that preceded it. She built a monastery where prayers could be offered for both kings, the slain and the slayer; and she did this at Gilling, in Yorkshire, the site of the murder. Bede has no more to say in condemnation of Oswiu, a greater king than Oswine, for whom he felt much respect as the man who saved his people from Penda, as well as on other, religious, grounds.[67] Oswiu, however, was not a saintly king, and Oswine was. It was at Tynemouth, where he was buried, and not at Gilling that the cult of Oswine seems later to have thrived.[68] Possession of the king's body was what counted in the long run.

I have made a group of Edwin, Oswald, and Oswine to indicate one category of king in which Bede had a special interest. All three may well have been popular rulers, and two were certainly successful in a material sense; but the personal virtues that Bede emphasizes are more technical than they look; they correspond to the requirements of the Church: protection, endowment, largesse, the prosecution of Christian warfare, and, above all, obedience to its teaching. But what all three kings had most

[65] Cf. Gregory of Tours's account of the fate of Bishop Praetextatus of Rouen, when charged before King Chilperic that 'contra utilitatem suam populis munera daret' (*Hist. Lib.* v. 18).

[66] *Hist. Eccl.* iii. 14.

[67] Ibid. 24.

[68] See Plummer, ii. 164. It seems to me that there is no compelling reason for preferring Collingham to Gilling as the scene of the assassination (cf. *V.C.H., Yorks., N. Riding*, i. 72, and *English Place-Name Society*, v. 288); nor did it seem so to Colgrave, *Earliest Life of Gregory the Great*, p. 40.

obviously in common was violent death in circumstances that could give them some claim to sanctity through martyrdom. Their cults originated in the manner of their deaths without necessarily producing quick results. We cannot tell, indeed, when any of the cults became firmly established; Oswine's may have been long after Bede's time. Bede was indicating one way in which English kings had achieved sanctity, thereby becoming useful to their successors: a group of royal saints, quite apart from their example, could add much prestige to a dynasty. Alcuin also, using Bede and the York traditions he had grown up in, thought it natural to make a little group of the great Northumbrian kings in his poem on the Church of York. But he thinks more highly of Oswiu than Bede did. The poem is important because Alcuin was an acknowledged expert on the kingly office. He was listened to with respect by Anglo-Saxons and Carolingians alike. Edwin he sees as the *rex pius*,[69] *largus in omnes* and *patriae pater*;[70] *sanctissimus* Oswald, also *patriae tutator*, is *moribus egregius, pauperibus largus, iudiciis verax, hastibus horribilis*, the benefactor of churches, and the worker of miracles.[71] Oswiu is *invictus bellis,* and also *pius, omnibus aequus*.[72] The kingly virtues were all there, in retrospect.

I turn now to a rather different group, the monk-kings; I mean those kings who resigned, or planned to resign, their temporal power in order to end their days as monks or pilgrims. Some resigned after long reigns, others much sooner, and a few abandoned their claims to rule before they had been made good. These were the men who took the teaching of the Church to its logical conclusion; but not the teaching of the Church on kingship, which certainly never envisaged resignation as a proper ambition for kings, though it might well be considered a possible consequence of the teaching that kingship was an office; for an office can be resigned. In this sense resignation was an unkingly act, and those who took the step owed any sanctity they might acquire not to their royal careers but to what happened afterwards, when they were private men. However, they too gave tone

---

[69] *MGH Poet. Lat. Caro. Aevi*, i, p. 173, v. 166.
[70] Ibid., p. 172, vv. 115–21.
[71] Ibid., p. 175, vv. 265–74.
[72] Ibid., p. 182, vv. 565–72.

to their dynasties and could be looked up to by their successors. Bede saw the matter thus, was proud of the kings whom the spiritual teaching of the Church had moved to resignation, and took no account of the political difficulties that might be created by an unlooked-for vacancy or the disappearance of a king with a reputation for strong rule or military prowess, old though he might be.

We may take some instances from the *Ecclesiastical History*. Oswiu, conqueror of Penda[73] and chairman at Whitby, resolved on his death-bed that if he recovered he would go to Rome to end his days 'ad loca sancta', for such, says Bede, was the affection he felt for the Roman see.[74] Nor is this surprising when one looks again at Bede's account of the synod of Whitby, to which he attached the greatest importance; for what settled the disciplinary issues under discussion there had not been the exact presentation of an argued case but the realization by Oswiu himself of the role of St. Peter. His words as Bede gives them were: 'I tell you that he [St. Peter] is the door-keeper, whom I have no wish to cross; as far as my knowledge and ability allow me, I shall obey him in every way, in case, when I reach the gates of the kingdom of heaven, there should be no one to open them, the keeper of the keys being my enemy.'[75] I suppose he would have envisaged a mighty key such as St. Peter bears on the coffin of St. Cuthbert made at Lindisfarne in 698, and now in Durham:[76] a real key, at any rate, and a real kingdom inside a formidable gate. Through St. Peter, Rome was the mistress of kings, and by St. Peter alone could they gain access to the kingdom of heaven. Whitby was a great victory for Roman teaching directed at kings, or at least it is so in Bede's account. Bede also inserts in his history a letter dispatched to Oswiu by Pope Vitalian.[77] Much debated by historians for its words about the succession to Canterbury, it contains other matter, which Alcuin considered useful enough to appropriate.[78] 'Blessed is the people',

[73] *Hist. Eccl.* iii. 24.
[74] Ibid. iv. 5.
[75] Ibid. iii. 26. For Bede's own teaching on the subject, see his sermon *In cathedra S. Petri* (ed. Hurst, *Corp. Christ.* cxxii, pt. iii, pp. 141–7, *Hom.* i. 20).
[76] See Battiscombe, *Relics of St. Cuthbert*, plate V.
[77] *Hist. Eccl.* iii. 29.
[78] *MGH Epist.* iv, p. 84, no. 41.

writes the pope, 'that is found worthy of so wise a king (*regem sapientissimum*) and worshipper of God, whom he does not worship alone, since day and night he works for the conversion of all his subjects to the Catholic and apostolic faith, to the redemption of his own soul. . . . Your people have believed in Christ the almighty God according to the words of the divine prophets [which he then cites]. . . . Your highness should therefore, as a member of Christ, in all things continually observe the rule (*piam regulam*) of the prince of the apostles. . . . We have ordered blessed gifts of the holy martyrs . . . to be delivered to you. . . . Truly your highness seeks and will obtain that all your islands shall be subjected to you, as I myself wish.' Vitalian invites obedience to St. Peter as a condition of a prosperous reign and an extension of power.

Oswiu reigned for nearly thirty years before he thought of resignation. Sebbi of the East Saxons also reigned for thirty years, but thought of the monk's life much earlier.[79] He was, says Bede, resuming a written source, 'Deo devotus', much given to religious works and preferring the monastic life to his kingly honours; indeed, he would long since have become a monk if only his queen had permitted a divorce. Therefore it was commonly said that a man so disposed would have made a better bishop than king; from which I infer that Bede was clear in his mind that a king whose behaviour approximated to that of a bishop was not necessarily doing his job properly. However, in his final illness Sebbi had his way and became a monk, distributing his treasure to the poor. In other words, he resigned, and then died to the accompaniment of a miracle, his stone coffin adjusting itself to his height. Cadwalla of the West Saxons and Ine his successor both retired to Rome,[80] Cadwalla after a reign of only two years. Aldhelm, who presumably knew him, described him as a great warrior,[81] and others before Dr. Bright may well have considered that he deserted his post. But Bede did not say so. He describes the king's reception in Rome with some pride and cites his Roman epitaph. Ine, however, reigned for thirty-seven years before following in his steps. Bede knew nothing, or what

[79] *Hist. Eccl.* iv. 11
[80] Ibid. v. 7.
[81] Plummer, ii. 278, cites the poem.

amounts to nothing, about **Ine**; he is silent about his legislation in which the grip of the Church can be seen tightening in practical ways upon the business of West Saxon life; silent, too, about his military activity. Nor would one guess from Bede that Ine had been to Glastonbury[82] what Dagobert was to St. Denis, as well as a benefactor of Malmesbury and Abingdon and founder of the bishopric of Sherborne, which he gave to his friend, Aldhelm.[83] Either Bishop Daniel of Winchester had had little to report to Bede on Ine, or it had seemed irrelevant to the historian. What Bede knew about Ine that he cared to report was simply this: Ine resigned his kingdom 'ac iuvenioribus commendato', and made his way to Rome as a pilgrim, 'quo familiarius a sanctis recipi mereretur in caelis'. He does not know that Ine was remembered and honoured in Rome as a saint;[84] perhaps no such report had reached England at the time when he was writing. What mattered to Bede was that Ine had resigned his kingdom into younger hands and followed Cadwalla to Rome. Yet another pair were King Cenred of the Mercians and Offa of the East Saxons.[85] Cenred, he says, had ruled for some time *nobilissime*,[86] and then 'nobilius multo regni sceptra reliquit'. He became a monk. His companion on the journey to Rome was Offa, not yet a king but heir to a kingdom. And here at last Bede sounds a note of regret: the handsome young Offa was missed by his people, who had seen in him the makings of a splendid king. But he had resigned all hope of his kingdom as well as his possessions, his wife, and his kindred, to go to Rome with Cenred, there to become a monk. He had been right to do so, in Bede's opinion, for his soul's sake. Old Ine was perhaps no loss, Offa was. Then, too, there was Æthelred of the Mercians, about whose reign Bede had plenty to say, adding, however, that Æthelred resigned his kingdom to Cenred and became a monk after a long

[82] J. Armitage Robinson, 'The Saxon abbots of Glastonbury', *Somerset Historical Essays* (1921), p. 35.

[83] On Ine's charters, the authenticity of which is disputed, see Sawyer, *Anglo-Saxon charters*, pp. 131–4. H. P. R. Finberg, 'Sherborne, Glastonbury and the expansion of Wessex', *Lucerna* (1964), pp. 95–116, is less sceptical than most scholars.

[84] *Acta Sanct.*, Feb., i, pp. 905–14.

[85] *Hist. Eccl.* v. 19.

[86] See Bede's account of how he tried to convert and instruct an impenitent follower, ibid. 13.

reign.[87] He went not to Rome but to Bardney, of which he had been a benefactor though probably not the founder. Bede gives no clue.[88] Hamilton Thompson concluded that Bede could not be acquitted of 'encouraging a dangerous habit',[89] which others might follow. Perhaps one can see a consequence of this in Bede's own complaint to Bishop Ecgberht of York about the proliferation of bogus monasteries; it was royal grants that had been responsible for these.[90] Royal enthusiasm for monasticism had its drawbacks.

Bede's exemplary kings were a quite considerable body of men, in stature and in number. King Ceolwulf, familiar with their careers, ended his life as a monk at Lindisfarne after a troubled reign.[91] Yet these kings were not in Bede's eyes a homogeneous body; their virtues differed; some achieved sanctity of a kind through good works or Christian victories, others through resignation, others again through martyrdom. But the impression he means to leave is clear enough. He is interpreting their actions in terms of traditional royal virtues as taught by the Fathers; virtues of the Church, some taken over from classical antiquity. A king who had them could expect prosperity and victory as well as his own salvation. Experts were at hand to explain the duties of a king's office; nor would the prestige of his blood or the traditions of his dynasty be weakened by his paying attention to what they taught. The new kind of Christian ruler could still fight his enemies and reward faithful service as in the past, unless indeed he were called to the ultimate distinction of the monastic life.

This picture could be filled out by consideration of other kings upon whose actions Bede commented in passing; and queens as well as kings. His pages are packed with material on royal ladies whose contribution to the slow process of national conversion was vital: Bertha, Æthelberg, Eorcongota, Ælfflaed, Eanfled, Æthelthryth, Hild, Hereswith, and Sexburh were some of them.

[87] Ibid. 19 and 24. Cf. Stenton, *Preparatory to Anglo-Saxon England* (1970), p. 181.
[88] Colgrave, *Earliest Life*, p. 14.
[89] *Bede, his life, times and writings*, p. 90.   [90] Ed. Plummer, i. 414.
[91] It was not only the troubles that made Bede doubtful about the future of Northumbria but also, as Mr. Campbell points out ('Bede', p. 172), because God's judgement had not yet been given.

There were women as distinguished and as influential abroad; but the list is still impressive. It is impressive in two ways: first, for their influence upon their husbands' courts, and secondly for their political power exercised as abbesses of great houses. No one could question the authority of Hild as Bede portrays her,[92] and Æthelthryth was a royal saint in whose honour he could write a hymn.[93] The list is impressive; but it still comprises only a small proportion of the princesses of the seventh and eighth centuries; and this may be why Bede makes so much of them as exemplars. His picture suggests some ways in which a queen might support the role of a Christian king. She might help to convert him from paganism, as queens had done since the time of the Empress Helena; she might assist clergy at his court, as St. Wilfrid was assisted,[94] by using her influence as far afield as the court from which she had come as a bride, or by gifts; she might bring up a strong line of kings. If she declined to live with her husband and entered a monastery, her political influence was no less on that account, though it was different in kind. Bede grasps the importance of queens but cannot analyse their role in the light of any patristic guidance: *regina* does not appear in Isidore's *Etymologiae*. His surest guide was the correspondence of Gregory the Great. He must have known that canonical restriction of the degrees of marriage customary among barbarians was irksome to kings; he certainly knew that ecclesiastical prohibition of marriage between a king and his stepmother, his predecessor's widow, was more than irksome; it could endanger a dynasty.[95] In these and other ways the Church made life hard for kings, even though there were compensating advantages. True, Bede lacked any English example of a powerful queen-regent, such as the Ostrogoth Amalasuntha, or Brunechildis and Balthildis in Francia; but the virtues required by such queens were precisely those of kings. The Church, still somewhat equivocal about kings, lacked any definition of the role of queens

[92] e.g. in *Hist. Eccl.* iv. 23. Stenton remarks (*Anglo-Saxon England*, p. 162) that 'no woman in the middle ages ever held a position comparable with that of Hild of Whitby'. This is certainly true of England.

[93] *Hist. Eccl.* iv. 20.

[94] By Eanfled; *Vita Wilf.*, chs. 2 and 3.

[95] Eadbald actually married Æthelberht's widow: *Hist. Eccl.* ii. 5. There are notable instances in Lombardic and Visigothic history.

beyond what was required of all Christian wives. Bede does his best with examples. Queens are the wives and the mothers of kings, and often the daughters, too. Clearly he feels that the Church must think in terms of dynasties; it must protect and perpetuate royal kindreds; it must educate royal children and see that they are instructed in the objects of good rule; it must pray for all of royal blood, living and dead. The royal kindred as a unit seems to invite a Christian terminology of its own.

If kings could benefit materially from obedience to the Church's teaching, they could equally come to grief by ignoring it. Edwin's successors, Osric and Eanfrid, lapsed into paganism and in consequence lost their kingdom.[96] Worse than that, the annalists of the Church had agreed—and it is important that agreement was possible—to assign the single year of their reign to their successor, Oswald, and to blot out all memory of the *reges perfidi*.[97] Bede thus gives a formidable example of the power of the Church over kings who were being encouraged to cherish the memory of their ancestors in written as well as oral record. The sons of King Saberht of Essex reverted to paganism. Bede tells a pretty story about this;[98] and he proceeds to indicate the consequence: they were not unpunished, for they and their army were slain in battle by the Gewissae. King Cenwalh of the West Saxons got rid of two successive bishops.[99] The result was that he found himself 'gravissimis regni sui damnis saepissime ab hostibus adflictus', and he concluded that, as he had once lost his throne through infidelity and had regained it by receiving the faith, so now his kingdom had lost divine protection because it had no bishop. Accordingly he sent for another bishop and did much better. The East Saxon king, Sigeberht, was murdered by those who could not stand his weakness in overlooking the claims of blood feud;[100] but Bede, who regretted the fate of the good king, yet saw in it the judgement of God on one who had disobeyed his bishop by entering the house of an excommunicate, even though he had subsequently abased himself before the

[96] *Hist. Eccl.* iii. 1.
[97] As D. P. Kirby points out—'Bede and Northumbrian chronology', *Engl. Hist. Rev.* lxxviii (1963), p. 515—this is good evidence for early king-lists.
[98] *Hist. Eccl.* ii. 5.
[99] Ibid. iii. 7.
[100] Ibid. 22.

bishop. Ecgfrith of Northumbria met his fate at the great battle of Nechtansmere[101] for no other reason than that, in the preceding year, he had authorized an expedition against the blameless, friendly Irish, who had prayed to God for vengeance: 'ocius Domino vindice poenas sui reatus luerent.' They got it.

Yet other kings, not specifically commended for their sanctity, earn good marks in passing. King Æthelwald of Northumbria gave land for a monastery to Bishop Cedd, so that he himself might often go there to pray and hear the scriptures, and ultimately be buried, 'nam et se ipsum fideliter credidit multum iuvari eorum orationibus cotidianis, qui illo in loco Domino servirent'.[102] Good in a different way was another Northumbrian, Alhfrith, friend and supporter of Wilfrid.[103] In his metrical Life of St. Cuthbert, Bede completes his account of the saint's prophecy about King Ecgfrith with a reference to Ahlfrith, his successor:

> Utque Novus Josia fideque animoque magis quam
> Annis maturus, nostrum regit inclitus orbem.[104]

It was precisely this image of Josiah that was soon to be associated with Charlemagne. Alhfrith was 'vir in scripturis doctissimus',[105] and, more than that, 'undecumque doctissimo'.[106] He listened attentively to Dryhthelm's account of his visit to the next world; and also he accepted a copy of Adomnan's book on the Holy Places, 'ac per eius est largitionem etiam minoribus ad legendum contraditus'.[107] He is one of Bede's few learned kings; it was a class with a future. If the letter of Abbot Ceolfrid to the Pictish king Naitan (of whom Bede certainly thought well)[108] is from

---

[101] *Hist. Eccl.* iv. 26.

[102] Ibid. iii. 23.

[103] Ibid. v. 19.

[104] *Bedas metrische Vita sancti Cuthberti*, ed. Werner Jaager (Leipzig, 1935), p. 100.

[105] *Hist. Eccl.* iv. 27.

[106] Ibid. v. 12.

[107] Ibid. 15.

[108] Ibid. 21. Plummer attributes the letter to Bede himself, but C. W. Jones, *Bedae Opera de Temporibus* (Cambridge, Mass., 1943), p. 104, disagrees. Levison leaves the matter open ('Bede as historian', in *Bede, his Life, Times and Writings*, p. 139; *Aus rheinischer und fränkischer Frühzeit*, p. 372). In any case, it is unlikely that Bede would have disagreed with the sentiments expressed.

Bede's pen, we have his explicit approval of the Lactantian, and
ultimately Platonic, statement of the role of a king: 'the world
would be most happy if kings were philosophers or philosophers
were kings . . . the more powerful men are in this world, the more
they should labour to know the commands of the supreme judge,
and by example and authority to induce those beneath them to
observe those commands, as they do themselves.' His brother-
Northumbrian, Alcuin, was soon to echo this in a letter to
Charlemagne: 'As the Platonic proverb has it, kingdoms would
be happy if philosophers, *id est amatores sapientiae*, reigned, or
kings studied philosophy . . . for it is *sapientia* that exalts the
humble and puts down the mighty.'[109] And in the Northumbrian
Annals,[110] under the year 800, we find: Charlemagne 'understood
how happy the state would be if ruled by *studiosi sapientiae*
or by kings who studied *sapientia*'.[111] It was, of course, a specific
type of *sapientia,* namely Christian *sapientia* expounded by the
Fathers, that the Northumbrians had in mind. For here, as
always, we have to remember that Church-writers used common
words with technical meanings. Nowhere is this clearer than in
Bede's famous résumé of the happy days when Theodore was
archbishop.[112] These were, he writes, of all times since the English
came to Britain, *feliciora tempora;* 'for their kings, *fortissimos
Christianosque,* were a terror to all barbarous peoples, and the
thoughts of all were bent upon the joys of the heavenly kingdom, of which they had lately heard; and whoever wished to
learn the scriptures had masters at hand to teach them'. It was
a very traditional picture of earthly *felicitas*: the mission of the
powerful Christian king was to assail his external enemies with
terror, and within his kingdom to encourage the spread of
Christian instruction by protecting its teachers. This, and not
the division of dioceses or the calling of synods, was what for
Bede constituted the *felicitas* of Theodore's time.

So far as I know, no English manuscript of Bede's day contains a picture of an English king; nor is there any reason why

[109] *MGH Epist.*, iv, no. 229, p. 373. See also no. 121, p. 177.
[110] On which see P. Hunter Blair, 'Some observations on the *Historia Regum*
attributed to Symeon of Durham', *Celt and Saxon: Studies in the Early British
Border* (1963), pp. 93 ff.
[111] Symeon of Durham, *Opera Omnia*, vol. ii, p. 64.
[112] *Hist. Eccl.* iv. 2.

there should be any. We must wait till the tenth century before
we have a picture of King Athelstan presenting a book to the
see of St. Cuthbert.[113] We know, indeed, how in Bede's lifetime
the scriptorium of St. Augustine's, Canterbury, depicted the
anointed King David composing his psalms, but the artist was
using a foreign model which showed David as prophet rather
than king.[114] Nor is there any representation in stone. G. F.
Browne once suggested that the falconer on the Bewcastle cross
was King Alhfrith,[115] doubtless influenced by the runic inscription above, which appears to mean that the cross had been
erected to the memory of the king by members of his following.[116] There are difficulties about the figure, but it is likelier to be
St. John with his eagle than Alhfrith with a hawk.[117] The same
scholar believed that a fragment of a cross-arm at Winwick
represents the dismemberment of the body of King Oswald.[118]
Whether or not Winwick can rightly claim to have had special
connections with Oswald, the dismemberment is more probably
'the massacre of the innocents with the typical iconography of
two men holding a small child by the legs'.[119] So that we have no
picture of any kind of an English king of the seventh or eighth
centuries. However, this does not mean that the age left no
picture of how it saw a king of another kind; it was fond of drawing and carving the *rex regum*, God the Father or Son, whose
authority was best reproduced in Christian iconography as regal.
For Bede, as for his sources, God was above all else a king when
the nature of his authority was in question; heaven was a kingdom. Some of the best representations of God as king are closely
associated with Bede's own monastery; for example, the Christ in
Majesty of Abbot Ceolfrid's gift-volume, the Codex Amiatinus,
who in some ways suggests a throned temporal king; and the
Christs of the Bewcastle and Ruthwell crosses, both of which

[113] Corpus Christi College, Cambridge, MS. 183 (frontispiece). Cf. M. R.
James, 'The manuscripts of Bede', *Bede, his Life, Times and Writings*, p. 234.
[114] In the Vespasian Psalter, fo. 30v, reproduced in D. H. Wright's edition
as frontispiece (*Early English Manuscripts in Facsimile*, Copenhagen, 1967).
[115] *The Venerable Bede, his Life and Writings* (1919), p. 79.
[116] Cf. G. Baldwin Brown, *The Arts in Early England*, v (1921), pp. 316, 244 ff.
[117] Ibid., p. 133. See also Rosemary Cramp, 'Early Northumbrian sculpture',
Jarrow Lecture (1965), p. 8.
[118] *The Venerable Bede*, p. 54.
[119] Miss Rosemary Cramp, in a letter to the writer.

Miss Rosemary Cramp associates with Jarrow.[120] They are commanding, victorious figures and, coming from the chisels of Jarrow craftsmen, afford some idea of how Bede himself conceived that God should be portrayed for general inspection. They seem to incapsulate, as nothing else does, the lesson of his teaching as exegete and historian. One may summarize it thus: earthly kings are in one respect, the exercise of power, a reflection of the heavenly king; this power they exercise by God's authority and for his purposes, namely the furthering of religion by protecting his priests and monks, encouraging their work, exhorting the faithful by personal example, and by carrying the Gospel, by fire and sword if necessary, into neighbouring territories where it was unknown or misunderstood. It is this that binds together a people into a *Populus Dei* after the manner of the Israelites. It is this that will bring them felicity, prosperity, good harvests, and victory over their enemies. One begins to see that the barbarian king might find his role in such a design without losing too much of what was traditional to him. Such, at least, was the argument of the *Ecclesiastical History*.

[120] 'Early Northumbrian sculpture', p. 8. For the illustrations to the Codex Amiatinus see R. L. S. Bruce-Mitford, 'The art of the Codex Amiatinus', *Journal of the Archaeological Association*, third series, xxxii (1969).

V

CHARLEMAGNE AND OFFA

In the middle and later eighth century we move into an age of fairly sophisticated thinking about kingship; sophisticated because evolved by well-read churchmen who knew how to write. At first glance, what they have to tell us may seem rather vaguely connected with what kings were in fact like and actually did. But this impression is deceptive. The annalists, for example, were often in close touch with royal courts. Their use of emotive political words could well bear examination. But it would require more than the length of a lecture to do justice to such a study. The writings we must consider were entirely practical in aim; they were addressed to kings well able to understand what they were being told; and their effects were immediate and far-reaching, if not always what had been intended. Ideals of kingship are presented with remorseless persistence to men who were every bit as much warriors as their predecessors; indeed, on a bigger scale. The scene is military.[1]

The event that marks its opening is the incursion of the Arabs in southern and central Francia. Bede lived long enough to weigh up what this might mean for Europe, and to record in a single sentence the completion of the long mental process that led him from tolerance of the Muslim presence in the Roman world through indifference to repugnance and alarm.[2] He may have had news of the battle of Poitiers, or of some other Frankish or Aquitanian victory over Arab raiders.[3] He does not attribute the victory, wherever it was, to divine intervention or see in it any special Christian destiny for the Frankish warlords; it was just

[1] How military, is brilliantly shown by F. L. Ganshof, *Frankish Institutions under Charlemagne* (Providence, Rhode Island, 1968), esp. ch. 2.

[2] I have attempted a sketch of this process in 'Bede's Europe', *Jarrow Lecture* (1962).

[3] See D. H. Wright, *Anglia*, lxxxii (1964), p. 114; and R. Latouche, *Gaulois et Francs* (Paris, 1965), p. 303.

a 'gravissima Sarracenorum lues' which was dealt with as *perfidia* deserved to be. But to some of his Frankish contemporaries in the entourage of the victorious Carolingians, things looked different. They interpreted the series of campaigns against the Arabs as Christian victories, and Charles Martel's Franks as a new Chosen People. How they reached this conclusion is uncertain, but it is clear enough, as Erdmann long ago showed,[4] that they are the fathers of the idea of crusade. To the continuator of Fredegar's chronicle, writing under the immediate eye of the Carolingians, Charles prevailed *Christo auxiliante*.[5] The sense of Frankish mission is intensified under Charles's son, Pippin III. It is reflected in the proud sentences of the prologue to *Lex Salica* composed during his reign;[6] in the revised *missa pro principe*, a liturgical statement of parallelism between Old Testament kingship and that of the Franks;[7] and in the earliest *Laudes Regiae*,[8] with their invocation of the soldier-like qualities of Christ and king alike. 'More than in any other Western Church ritual, an extraordinary space is granted, in the Gallic and Frankish sacramentaries, to the liturgical hallowing of weapons, standards, army and ruler.'[9] Liturgy of this type was 'in the last resort the business of the king',[10] and it would be wide of the mark to represent this martial liturgifying of the king, any more than his unction, as a smart move by the Church to capture kingship and make of it something that a king and his warriors would not approve, if they understood it. We shall not again be free from the reiterated claim that the Carolingians were the reincarnation of the Old Testament kings; and it is rather more than the holding-up to kings of biblical exemplars, already familiar in Merovingian times. It signifies the promotion of the whole Frankish people to a new rank: that of the New Israel, destined to save Christian society in the west. Such is the tone of many a papal

[4] *Die Entstehung des Kreuzzugsgedankens* (Stuttgart, 1935), ch. 1.
[5] Ed. B. Krusch, *MGH Script, Rer. Mero.* ii. 175; ed. J. M. Wallace-Hadrill, *The Fourth Book of the Chronicle of Fredegar with its Continuations* (1960), p. 91.
[6] Cf. Ewig, *Das Königtum*, pp. 41–5.
[7] Ewig, ibid., p. 44, n. 168, sees a possibility that it belongs to Charles Martel's lifetime.
[8] Kantorowicz, *Laudes Regiae*, pp. 15–60.
[9] Ibid., p. 30.
[10] Ibid., p. 60.

letter: not only their kings but the Franks themselves are different from other Germanic peoples, different in calling and role. This is explicit in the unction of Pippin III in 751, and again in 754. Not only Pippin and his family is chosen and anointed for a special task; a people also is chosen, having *utilitas* and *potestas* of a military kind. Too much time is spent in arguing over what can be called the constitutional implications of Pippin's unction. What the popes got from it is clear enough: protection for Rome and her patrimony. But for the Franks, this mattered little beside the gain of a king whom they wanted and had themselves proposed. They did not see him as a different kind of king because anointed but only as a stronger one, as a specially-commissioned warlord with a power unequalled since the days of Dagobert. The change of dynasty from Merovingian to Carolingian implied a union of king and people in a single purpose. Unction does not separate Pippin from his Franks and set him above them in a position determined by the Church alone; it identifies him with them in the common task of the prosecution of Frankish Christianity on the field of battle. Those who drew attention to the parallel between him and the Old Testament kings would not have missed the point that Saul was made king of Israel by Samuel because of imminent military crisis: that was why the Israelites had wanted him.

So much I say by way of preface. Outside pressures had brought back to much of western Europe the need for great warlords; and this was soon to affect England too. They were pressures felt by all, churchmen included. Nobody expected the new David to confine himself to his harp. Just what he was meant to do was never set out in detail in the lifetimes of Charles Martel and Pippin. We have to wait till the reign of Charlemagne before much that was implicit became explicit in reasoned statements by those who knew. Among the first to make such statements were two Englishmen, Cathwulf and Alcuin; and it is hardly possible to understand the situation of kingship in their own country till some account has been taken of how their ideas were applied in practice by Charlemagne, to whom they addressed themselves. Both necessarily belonged to the insular tradition of the interpretation of kingship; that is to say, their thoughts were rooted in the Bible, in Pseudo-Cyprian's Twelve Abuses, and in Isidore. To Rome direct they owed little or nothing. Of the two, Alcuin is the more important by far; and so it is unavoidable to consider his views with some care.[11] These he expresses in his bulky correspondence (the English part of which I reserve till later). Whether we really have from him the earliest example of a Carolingian *speculum principis*, or mirror of princes,[12] is doubtful: it depends on what one thinks was the purpose of his rhetorical exercise known as the *Disputatio de rhetorica et de virtutibus*. But in all conscience there is enough in the letters.

In the first place Alcuin accepted the by now traditional view of the Frankish role in Christian society and of their kings. He was in no doubt that Charlemagne's position, irrespective of whether he were king or emperor, was unlike that of any other western ruler. It was not his unction that gave him this special role, for other kings were also anointed, but his evident election by God to carry out special duties of which Rome approved. Alcuin took the great king as he found him; and what he found was a warrior of the first rank who was prepared to interpret his own actions, inside Francia and also outside, in a Christian sense. Alcuin provides a running commentary on what happens before his eyes. This he does in an atmosphere of friendship with the king; no one who reads his letters can question the existence of a personal bond. Yet it is also friendship of a special kind. It is *amicitia* founded in *eruditio*.[13] From Alcuin's point of view, as a scholar, Charlemagne's first business was to be learned in the Catholic faith, to teach it and see that it was taught and understood. The king was *doctor* as well as *dux*. He could be addressed thus: 'O rex augusto clarissime dignus honore, et dux et doctor et decus imperii.'[14] Cathwulf thought that he should not confine his learning to the Catholic faith: 'ut sis in sapientia divina et saecularibus litteris inbutus sicut David et Salomon et ceteri

---

[11] I consider that the best book on Alcuin is still that of C. J. B. Gaskoin, *Alcuin: His Life and His Work* (1904), though valuable points are made by A. Kleinclausz, *Alcuin* (Paris, 1948), and E. S. Duckett, *Alcuin, Friend of Charlemagne* (New York, 1951).

[12] Such is the contention of L. Wallach, *Alcuin and Charlemagne* (Ithaca, New York, 1959), ch. iv; but it is disputed, I think reasonably, by Anton, *Fürstenspiegel*, pp. 87 ff.

[13] See W. Edelstein, *Eruditio und sapientia: Weltbild und Erziehung in der Karolingerzeit* (Freiburg im Br., 1965), pp. 42–169.

[14] *MGH Epist.* iv., *Karo. Aevi*, ii, p. 415, no. 257.

reges fuerunt.'[15] And this fits in well enough with the king's literary interests as Einhard portrays them,[16] as well as being pretty much in line with the classicizing tendencies of the Palace School as these can be inferred from its manuscripts still extant. As *doctor* and *magister* of his people, Charlemagne will lead them to salvation; this is what his *sagacitas, sapientia,* and *scientia* were for. Alcuin has in mind something more than a revival of interest in ancient learning, Christian or pagan. He wants the king to see himself as the creator of a new Christian community; he looks to the future and is no antiquarian. If we want donnish *eruditio* we have to wait a few years for Servatus Lupus of Ferrières, whose backward-looking learning was quite free from any thought of national salvation; such was not Alcuin's, nor Charlemagne's. Teaching, for them, meant salvation. Hence, Alcuin's objection to the imposition of tithe on the newly conquered and converted Saxons: the king must first teach and only exact tithe when the new converts understood their place in Christian society. His appeal had nothing to do with soft-heartedness.

Eruditio was the special concern of Alcuin, on which he could be expected to say something. What he said, however, did not run counter to Charlemagne's own inclinations: learning had a social purpose and the king felt responsible for it. Alcuin's letters give no systematic analysis of what the king should be doing—still less why he should be doing it. But his scattered opinions can be summarized like this:[17] the king's authority is characterized by *potestas, sapientia,* and *praedicatio*; his aim should be the subjugation of *inimicos gentes* everywhere through the *terror* he inspires by his military power; to his own people he is protector, judge, guide, and preacher; and the outcome of good rule will be earthly *felicitas,* the peace and prosperity of his Christian subjects. Much of this is traditional in detail. Yet it is more. It lets us see in what sense Charlemagne had a sacral function, however derived: he was a *praedicator* and a *doctor,* but not a *sacerdos.* If he was a priest-king, it was in no sacramental sense but as a teacher and a protector of those who

---

[15] *MGH Epist.* iv, *Karo Aevi,* ii, p. 503, no. 7.
[16] *Vita Karoli Magni,* ch. 25 (ed. Holder-Egger, p. 26).
[17] As, in effect, does Wallach, *Alcuin and Charlemagne,* p. 17.

taught; a protector, moreover, who wielded a sword. Because of this he was more like David than Melchisedech. Happy the people, writes Alcuin, that has such a king: 'et gladium triumphalis potentiae vibrat in dextera et catholicae praedicationis tuba resonat in ligua. Ita et David. . . .'[18] Each in his day was the prophetic leader of a Chosen People, a missionary with a sword and a trumpet. Only in this sense was Charlemagne the *rector ecclesiae*. Alcuin and his contemporaries were not at all bothered by any Gelasian implication of division of temporal and spiritual power.[19] It is thus that the external aspect of the king's power engages Alcuin; the fact of constant warfare against Saxons, Avars, and Muslims fitted into a pattern of thought about Christian kingship. Others would have agreed with him. The fathers of the synod of Frankfurt, for example, saw Charlemagne primarily as a triumphant Christian warrior whose victories over external enemies were victories for *pax* and *libertas ecclesiae*;[20] and Paulinus of Aquilea chose to express a purely Christian objective in military terms, thus: 'Cristatis instructi galeis pergunt ad bella doctissimi.'[21] But there was also an internal aspect: the king's role in the society he did not have to conquer. Here especially Alcuin writes in a different tone to Charlemagne than to other kings; he can make assumptions about Charlemagne's grip on the kingly virtues that he cannot make elsewhere. Charlemagne does not need a mirror of princes; he is himself one.[22] He is a king who already understands that his relations with his own subjects must be governed by the need to exercise the power of *correctio*: 'Haec est, O dulcissime David, gloria laus et merces tua . . . ut diligentissime populum . . . corrigere studeas.'[23] He does not have to be told to do it: he already does it. What is this *correctio*? It is the duty of constant

[18] *MGH Epist.* iv, *Karo. Aevi*, ii, p. 84, no. 41.
[19] In a famous letter to the pope, Charlemagne distinguishes between his and the pope's functions within Christian society without seeking to demarcate the zones within which they operated (ibid., pp. 137 ff., no. 93).
[20] *MGH Conc.* ii, pp. 141 ff.
[21] *MGH Epist.* iv, *Karo, Aevi*, ii, pp. 518–19, no. 15.
[22] The point is made by Anton, *Fürstenspiegel*, p. 95, whose whole treatment of Alcuin's position deserves attention.
[23] *MGH Epist.* iv, *Karo. Aevi*, ii, p. 176, no. 121. It is argued by P. E. Schramm, *Kaiser, Könige und Päpste*, i (Stuttgart, 1968), pp. 302 ff., 337, that Charlemagne presided over a *correctio* rather than a 'renaissance'.

supervision of the moral life of a people; the punishment of those who go astray and the rewarding of the obedient; it is the meaning of the justice the king metes out; the domestic aspect of the *terror* he inspires in foreign enemies. So far, then, from the king being separated from his people by the divine grace that he uniquely enjoys, he seems to draw much nearer to them.[24] There is a paternalism about Carolingian rule that is lacking earlier. Charlemagne in particular is involved in a fatherly way in the lives of all his subjects—*subjecti* though they be. Not all of them liked it; it has its place in the history of opposition to the Carolingians which has yet to be written; but all were certainly alive to it. We may take the matter a step further by inquiring what the outcome of *correctio* would be in the hands of a vigilant king. What does Charlemagne achieve in his care for right order among his people and by constant harping upon the words *corrigere, emendare, meliorare, restituere, renovare, reformare, revocare*?[25] The answer is *pax*. It sounds a quixotic aim for a man who was almost always at war. But plainly it was his aim, and Alcuin and others have much to say about it. For their starting-point they took Augustine's famous sketch of the *imperator felix*. It took them to an emotional plane where they sometimes felt the need to express themselves in verse; and so, on occasion, they put their feelings about the new era of peace and concord, and of the man who presided over it, into what amount to hymns of praise.[26] Also from Alcuin's letters one could cull a large collection of passages illustrating his concept of *pax*: it is the condition achieved by a people that is God-centred;[27] together with *fides* it will give them unity;[28] whatever breaks this unity— heresy, for example, and schism—will land them in trouble.[29] But *pax* is not exclusively a spiritual concept: it is also social and political; and so it must be taught and preached.[30] The king and his great men must understand it as well as do bishops and monks.

[24] The contrary case, based on Ullmann's view of *gratia Dei*, is presented by Green, *Carolingian Lord*, pp. 223 ff.
[25] Cf. Schramm, *Kaiser, Könige und Päpste*, i, p. 330.
[26] Cf. Anton, *Fürstenspiegel*, p. 99.
[27] *MGH Epist.* iv, *Karo. Aevi*, ii, p. 363, no. 219.
[28] Ibid., p. 192, no. 129.
[29] Ibid., p. 54, no. 19.
[30] Ibid., p. 353, no. 212.

Above all, it is the Christian unity of Charlemagne's empire that in Alcuin's eyes gives it *pax, caritas*, and *concordia*. He tells the king that all should pray for the extension of his rule so that 'sanctae pacis et perfectae caritatis omnes ubique regat et custodiat unitas'.[31] The effect of this teaching on Charlemagne's legislation is obvious; and one can see why it attracted him. There was nothing in it to make him feel that intellectuals were trying to limit his power by defining its basis in a new sense, and no suggestion that he ought not to be fighting the enemies of Francia or interfering autocratically in the lives of his subjects. On the contrary, it gave him additional reasons for doing what he wanted to do by identifying his aims with God's purposes; and, moreover, it placed him firmly in a historical setting. In part, at least, Alcuin succeeded in striking the right note because he was an Englishman. He had the insular slant on kingship derived from close attention to Pseudo-Cyprian and Isidore as well as to the Old Testament. Thus, as he runs over in his mind the kingly virtues, *pietas* stands out among the rest, with its dependent virtues of *misericordia*, care for the Church, and protection of those without protectors. *Justitia* is swallowed up in *correctio*. Moreover, a hint of the pagan mystique of rule is allowed to creep in. A people's good luck, its success in war, good harvests, and freedom from plague are still to be associated with the way their king rules and how he comports himself. Natural phenomena will bear witness to this, presaging disaster if need be. The gist of this is summarized in a letter to an English king, but it will stand equally well for Charlemagne: 'Legimus quoque quod regis bonitas totius est gentis prosperitas, victoria exercitus, aeris temperies, terrae habundantia, filiorum benedictio, sanitas plebis . . . quia aequitas principum populi est exaltatio.'[32] (*Populi*, note, and not *subjectorum*.) Alcuin was immensely impressed by Charlemagne; behind his flattery lay the conviction that here at last was the great king required by Christian tradition. There was nobody else like him.

It would be easy to demonstrate how the pressure of this intellectual stimulus affected Charlemagne's practical decisions; and to some extent this has already been done by others. Here it will

[31] Ibid., p. 415, no. 257.
[32] Ibid., pp. 51 ff., no. 18.

be enough to draw attention to a few instances. In the first place, the circle of scholars at the king's court with their magnificent library were no mere whim on the king's part. They belonged to the structure of his own idea of kingship—a Davidic court of theologians, singers, poets, and warriors, who ate, bathed, and hunted together;[33] and to the same close company belonged his own family, the unity of which stands out as more significant to him than his affection for any particular member of it. Poetry and theology seemed proper kingly interests. Charlemagne was himself a singer—one in a great line of singers that included not only David but Achilles, Gelimer, Sisebut, Beowulf, Hrothgar, Merlin, and Alfred. It reflected something personal: his refusal to abandon the golden Frankish past. It belonged to the Christian present. When it came to the naming of his two sons born in 778, he remembered the Merovingians; not the most recent Merovingians, the adoption of whose names could have suggested a claim to dynastic continuity, but two of the great Merovingians of the distant past, Clovis and Chlotar.[34] His own rule had grown out of something historical—the tradition of Frankish military power. As lord of such a tradition he could find moral support from the court poets who hailed him as *pater Europae* and *pharus Europae*,[35] or acclaimed him as *heros* (a term they specially loved). All dictators need adulation; Charlemagne was a large-sized one. His poets reassured him that the Christian military empire he ruled was still that of the Franks.

[33] See J. Fleckenstein, 'Karl der Grosse und sein Hof', *Karl der Grosse, Lebenswerk und Nachleben*, i: *Persönlichkeit und Geschichte* (Düsseldorf, 1965), p. 49.
[34] On Charlemagne's intentions see E. Hlawitschka, 'Merowingerblut bei den Karolingern?', *Festschrift Tellenbach*, pp. 66–91, as against K. A. Eckhardt, 'Merowingerblut, I: die Karolinger und ihre Frauen', *Germanenrechte* N.F., *Deutschrecht. Archiv*, x (1965), p. 11; O. G. Oexle, 'Die Karolinger und die Stadt des heiligen Arnulf', *Frühmittelalterliche Studien*, i (1967), p. 270; and G. Tellenbach, 'Zur Bedeutung der Persönenforschung für die Erkenntnis des früheren Mittelalters', *Freiburger Universitätsreden*, N.F. xxv (1957), p. 21 and n. 57.
[35] See the poem *Karolus Magnus et Leo Papa*, MGH Poet. i, pp. 366–79; also *Ein Paderborner Epos vom Jahre 799* (Paderborn, 1966) ed. H. Beumann, F. Brunhölzl, and W. Winkelmann, for what may be called the Aachen view of Charlemagne's Christian-Germanic high-kingship blending into emperorship. Recent work on Charlemagne has now been acutely evaluated by D. A. Bullough, 'Europae Pater', *Engl. Hist. Rev.* lxxxv (1970).

It can be argued that Charlemagne's insistence on obedience
and fidelity sprang from the special authority that he derived
from God, *gratia Dei*; for it was this that made his people
subjecti; and this is true in a sense. Yet I am more impressed by
his awareness of his people being one with him in religion than
I am by his being set apart from them. He ruled a community
of belief, or so he said. He was their *corrector* or reformer, which
is why he was attracted by the Israelite reformer, Josiah: 'circum-
eundo, corrigendo, ammonendo ad cultum veri Dei studuit
revocare.'[36] Plainly it was as a community of belief that the
popes, too, encouraged him to think of his empire. In their eyes
the community he ruled was Roman; from Rome he derived
much; and the emperors he looked back to were Christian-Roman
emperors. Even so, his imperial coronation marked an intensifica-
tion of feelings already active rather than any change in
approach to the duties of rule. In particular it marked an intensi-
fication of his insistence on *fidelitas*, with increased abhorrence
of its counterpart, *infidelitas*.[37] The capitulary called the
Admonitio Generalis of 789 is probably the clearest expression
of his claim to interfere *causa correctionis* in all the business of
Frankish life, though it antedates the imperial coronation by
eleven years. What is arresting about the *Admonitio* is not the
autocracy of the ruler nor the measures he envisages but his
reasons for envisaging them. From a mass of biblical and canonical citations and ecclesiastical directives what stands out most
clearly is the search for peace and concord: 'ut pax sit et concordia et unianimitas cum omni populo christiano inter ... omnes
ubique seu maiores seu minores personas'.[38] It is the condition of
collaboration between officials;[39] also it is the condition without
which the *populus* itself cannot move forward to salvation. There
must be no *invidia* or *odium* or *homicidia infra patriam* for any
reason—'nec causa ultionis nec avaritiae nec latrocinandi'. It is
the earliest piece of legislation against feud, against, that is, part
of the structure of Germanic society. Feud is not singled out for
special condemnation or branded as an inefficient way of settling

[36] *Admonitio Generalis, MGH Capit.* i, *praef.*, p. 54, no. 22.
[37] See Ewig, *Das Königtum*, p. 67.
[38] *MGH Capit.* i, p. 58, no. 22, cl. 62.
[39] As Ganshof notes, *Frankish Institutions*, p. 5.

differences; nor is there any condemnation of the monetary settlements that formed an essential part of the feuding process; it is merely one cause of *homicidia*, itself the plainest indication of a break-down of *concordia*. The *Admonitio* was a statement of intent. It never worked to any great extent; but the intentions outlined in it were never abandoned by Charlemagne. They recur in subsequent capitularies. In a word, Alcuin's programme was Charlemagne's, and he did what he could to implement it. It brought him nearer to his *populus*.

We may note one final point about the *Admonitio*. In chapter 70 the king insists that bishops shall satisfy themselves and him that their priests and those committed to them fully understood the words they used in worship, 'ut quisque sciat quid petat a Deo'. In fact, there must be clear vernacular explanation of the language of religion. As he put it in another context, he liked 'nudum sermonem nudamque litteram rem nudam signifi-cantem'.[40] And again, 'intelligant, bene intelligant'.[41] Clarity, understanding, require the use of the vernacular. As in liturgical explanation so in law and the business of life, Charlemagne up-grades the vernacular, of whatever kind.[42] It is fit to be spoken and written if it assists understanding, and so concord. If words are wrongly written or misunderstood they lose their effect; the names of things must accurately express their content, and in doing so they acquire a kind of mystical force of their own. More-over, vernacular is honourable, since it binds the Christian *populus* to its heroic past. Einhard was perfectly clear that this was Charlemagne's personal view. It was not shared by his successor.

The great man was already a legend in his own lifetime, and the ramifications of that legend were of the first importance throughout the middle ages.[43] Yet he had to wait till the twelfth century to achieve canonization, and then at the hands of an anti-pope. His cult, subsequently, was never more than local. No

[40] *MGH Epist.* iv, *Karo. Aevi*, ii, p. 552, no. 35.
[41] Ibid.
[42] See W. Betz, 'Karl der Grosse und die Lingua Theodisca', *Karl der Grosse*, ii, *Das geistige Leben*, pp. 300–6.
[43] Cf. the important studies of R. Folz, *Le Souvenir et la légende de Charle-magne* (Paris, 1950) and *Études sur le culte liturgique de Charlemagne* (Paris, 1951).

Carolingian saint's Life (and there are plenty of them) claims him for a saint, either of the Church or of the people. His remains at Aachen worked, so far as I know, no miracles. Yet Carolingian hagiography may still reflect something of him in its emphasis on obedience as a Christian duty, and on the need for fidelity.[44] He did almost all the right things, some to excess; and as Einhard sums him up in his idealizing way we can still detect the purposes of a real man behind the writer's catalogue of virtues: *prudentia, magnanimitas, amicitia, constantia, patientia, liberalitas,* and *moderatio.* They are all there—as traditional a list as one could wish for. Einhard gives examples of what these words meant in practice. He does not think that Charlemagne's practice of kingship was in all respects like that of his predecessors; neither does he think that it ought to have been. He would probably have said that Charlemagne's own family had listened overmuch to churchmen's ideas about rule; virtues were all very well in their way, but what really made a great king was *potentia* on the battlefield, and *magnanimitas*: these were what proved God's royal purpose. All in all, his picture of Charlemagne is carefully profane, in the sense that he shows his readers how a great layman can be as worthy of imitation as any miracle-worker of the sort dear to the popular western tradition that stemmed from the biography of St. Martin by Sulpicius Severus.[45] Einhard's Charlemagne passes the acid test: he has, and brings to his people, *fortuna,* good luck. The annalists noted it too.

Kingship in eighth-century England—post-Bede, at least—betrays symptoms of the same political unrest that lay behind the rise of the Carolingians. One should be chary of seeing direct influence of Francia on England, or the other way about, in this or any other matter, unless there is firm evidence for it. What one can see here is a political situation common to the two lands in which, with help from the Church, comparable ideas about kingship could develop. Mr. Eric John seems recently to have spotted something about the English Bretwaldas, notably the southern ones, the significance of which appears not to have been

---

[44] See Graus, *Volk, Herrscher und Heiliger,* pp. 355–60.
[45] This has been clarified by H. Beumann, 'Die Historiographie des Mittelalters als Quelle für die Ideengeschichte des Königtums', repr. in *Ideengeschichtliche Studien* (Darmstadt, 1962).

fully appreciated before.[46] It is perhaps going too far to see in Bede's seven Bretwaldas (as they were later called) a riposte to an indigenous tradition (preserved in Nennius) of seven British emperors;[47] but some of Bede's great kings can plausibly be seen as more than warlords and tribute-takers; they had an authority over the Church that overrode that of their subordinate kings; and this may be reflected in the titles with which churchmen sometimes greeted them or referred to them: for example, *imperator*[48] and *rex Anglorum*,[49] though there are perhaps too few of these to build on. More plainly it is reflected in a charter recording the Clovesho synod of 742, where King Æthelbald of Mercia confirms the privileges of the Kentish churches.[50] It is indeed 'the act of an overlord'[51] and suggestive also of the attitude of some Carolingian rulers when confirming church privileges in areas outside their immediate jurisdiction. The English over-lord, like the Frankish, can interfere in the affairs of the Church wherever his overlordship is acknowledged and whatever its basis. It was a weapon that the Church encouraged him to use, for, as we have seen, it liked overlords with military power commensurate with their authority. What better way was there of ensuring the stability of Church property and uniformity in Church teaching?

Now, there is this peculiarity about the overlords, Mercian and Frankish, of the later eighth century: they had learnt from their predecessors that too much land could be donated to churches.[52] It is characteristic of both that they were careful about donations; which is another way of saying that they saw the need not to impoverish their dynasties if anything like secure succession to their crowns were to be achieved. Particularly we can see this in

[46] *Orbis Britanniae* (1966), ch. 1. See also E. E. Stengel, 'Imperator und Imperium bei den Angelsachsen', in *Abhandlungen und Untersuchungen zur Geschichte des Kaisergedankens im Mittelalter* (Cologne, 1965).

[47] John, *Orbis Britanniae*, p. 12.

[48] As St. Boniface in a letter to Archbishop Cuthbert, presumably referring to King Æthelbald (ed. Tangl, p. 169, no. 78).

[49] e.g. Bede, *Hist. Eccl.* i. 32 (Gregory I to Æthelberht), ibid. ii. 10 (Pope Boniface to Edwin).

[50] Haddan and Stubbs, iii, pp. 340 ff.; Sawyer, *Anglo-Saxon Charters*, p. 89, no. 90.

[51] John, *Orbis Britanniae*, p. 17.

[52] Ibid., p. 22.

the case of the greatest Mercian, Offa; and he merits special attention.

To take the matter of Church property first: perhaps following the lead of Æthelbald, if Mr. John is right, Offa is clear that he alone can authorize the granting of land in perpetuity to churches. Charters seem to show this in his treatment of the lands of the Hwicce, the South Saxons, and the Kentings; it could be inferred for the more independent West Saxons, and conceivably for the East Angles.[53] No doubt this business of royal booking could have covered secular properties as well as ecclesiastical and also have strengthened Offa's hold over fyrd-service. Whether it did or not, here was an overlord who was not going to impoverish himself as Bede said the Northumbrian kings had. The Church at large may have acquired less new property in consequence; we cannot be sure; but certainly it gained added security for what it did hold. The king's new mastery may also appear in his royal titles in certain charters, and to this Stenton gave his attention in a famous article.[54] His argument was that titles in charters, so early, conveyed a degree of political meaning that could not be allowed to the bombastic titles of later centuries; and Offa's titles reflected a real change of circumstance. He is both *rex Merciorum* and *rex Anglorum*, and once, in 774, *rex totius Anglorum patriae*.[55] By coincidence it was also in 774 that Charlemagne enlarged his title to *rex Francorum et Langobardorum*, to correspond with realities.[56] Moreover, Offa is *rex a rege regum constitutus*;[57] his kingship owes something to God's approval, as indeed did that of several of his predecessors. Clearly he reigns *gratia Dei*. In an early charter—a grant to the bishop of Rochester in 764—he bears what may be the most revealing title of all: 'rex Merciorum, regali prosapia Merciorum oriundus atque omnipotentis Dei

---

[53] Ibid., pp. 23 ff.

[54] 'The supremacy of the Mercian kings', *Engl. Hist. Rev.* xxxiii (1918), pp. 433–52.

[55] Birch, *Cart. Sax.* i, p. 302, no. 214.

[56] The earliest example is *MGH Dipl. Karo.*, p. 114, no. 80. Reference may be made to my 'Charlemagne and England', *Karl der Grosse*, i, *Persönlichkeit und Geschichte*, pp. 683–98, where this and some of the following matters are considered.

[57] Haddan and Stubbs, iii, p. 483; Birch, *Cart. Sax.*, p. 381, no. 274.

dispensatione ejusdem constitutus in regem.'[58] The claim of blood has not been overlooked, but neither has the protection of God. The king was not concerned to say just how he had been 'constitutus in regem' by God, and his contemporaries may have been almost as much in the dark as we are. The fact remained that he was. Charter-titles will take us thus far but no further.

We may learn a little more from genealogies, with the assistance of Dr. Kenneth Sisam,[59] who has shown that written royal genealogies, as distinct from mere king-lists, cannot be traced further back than the eighth century and are closely associated with royal Mercian interests. Not all scholars would share his scepticism about earlier interest in and knowledge of genealogy; there is very little evidence; but in respect of the written genealogies that survive in manuscripts, he is unquestionably right. It is, in his own words, no chance that the famous Vespasian collection of royal English genealogies[60] 'can be traced to Mercia in the last decades of the eighth century, for then Mercian power was at its height under King Offa'.[61] It suited Offa to trace his hereditary title back to the kings of Angel, as tradition allowed, and to associate his genealogy with lists of popes and bishops that recalled his 'policy of playing a leading part in Church affairs'. How happy the Carolingians would have been with a genealogy one half as good as Offa's. Only the Merovingians could have competed at that game. Now, part of Offa's interest may have been to assist the claims of his son Ecgfrith (to whom I shall return); but this cannot be all. We should ask why Offa troubled himself with genealogies when his recent predecessors apparently did not. There may be two reasons. The first is that texts of the Bible, some very splendid, had a wider dissemination in the second half of the eighth century than in the first. One thinks of the magnificent Canterbury texts, of St. Chad's Gospels at Lichfield, and of the Irish MacRegol Gospels in Bodley.[62] St. Chad's Gospels may bring one into the neighbour-

[58] Birch, *Cart. Sax.* i, p. 276, no. 195.
[59] 'Anglo-Saxon royal genealogies', *Proc. Brit. Acad.* xxxix (1953).
[60] Brit. Mus., Cottonian MS. Vespasian B VI, fos. 104–9. Ed. Sweet, *The Oldest English Texts* (Early Engl. Text Soc., lxxxiii (1885), pp. 169 ff.).
[61] 'Anglo-Saxon royal genealogies', pp. 329, 330.
[62] P. McGurk, *Latin Gospel Books* (Paris, etc., 1961), pp. 31 and 40.

hood of Offa's own court, where it would be entirely reasonable to imagine a library and even a court school of sorts. Alcuin, after all, refers Offa to Bede's *History* for a letter of Pope Gregory, 'quae apud te scripta scimus'.[63] Offa may not have had any manuscript as grand as the Moore Bede, which may well at that very time have been in Charlemagne's library at Aachen,[64] but he had a good working manuscript of the same book known to Alcuin. Both kings, then, would almost certainly have been conversant with Bede's interpretation of kingship. The Bible has a recurrent concern with genealogy; we find it notably in the Old Testament but also in the New: St. Matthew starts with a genealogy of Christ the King, which in St. Chad's and the MacRegol Gospels is framed in colour to enhance its importance. In a word, the Bible is one possible guide to, and model for, royal genealogies. There is, however, a second reason why Offa and not his predecessor Æthelbald should have turned back to his ancestors. It helped to legitimize his rule at a time when it was challenged. It strengthened him in England and possibly further afield. He may well have looked with anxiety across the Channel at the mounting power and pretensions of the Carolingians, with whose rise as a royal dynasty his own reign almost exactly corresponds. Pippin III had been only six years king when Æthelbald died in 757; so that most of Pippin's reign, and most of Charlemagne's, was covered by Offa's reign in England.

This consideration brings us face to face with a relationship that may have most to reveal of Offa's idea of his own authority.[65] His commercial relations with the continent need not here concern us, not yet the issues of coinage that appear to have a connecion with them. Certainly these coins reveal something of Offa's power, and also of his intelligence, but nothing directly to the present purpose. His relations with Charlemagne moved on a more personal plane. They take shape in the context of royal unction. Charlemagne himself had been anointed at his father's wish by the pope; it was part of the deal that made the Carolingians at once patrons and clients of Rome, bound to each other in a family bond that may have looked for a model to the earlier

[63] Levison, *England and the Continent*, p. 245, citing Lehmann's text.
[64] B. Bischoff, 'Die Hofbibliothek Karls des Grossen', *Karl de Grosse*, ii, p. 56.
[65] What follows is largely a résumé of my 'Charlemagne and England'.

connection of the Eastern emperors with those kings they called their *filii*.[66] In his turn, Charlemagne sent his sons Pippin and Louis to Rome for papal unction in 781.[67] But Offa also was in touch with Rome. Three or four years later Pope Hadrian writes to Charlemagne[68] about a rumour that Charlemagne himself had reported to him, to the effect that Offa had approached Charlemagne with a proposal that the pope should be deposed and replaced by a Frankish candidate. It was, of course, the pope added, *incredibilis*, but still he was alarmed; if kings could lose their *ministeria*, so presumably could popes, at least in Offa's opinion. But why should Offa have been tempted to make such an approach? A possible solution lies in his bad relations with Archbishop Jaenberht of Canterbury and in his plan to anoint his only son, Ecgfrith. The hostile archbishop, perhaps supported by the pope, might have declined to officiate. It is a guess where only a guess will do. The subsequent papal mission to the English and the legatine synods (where Charlemagne's interest was unofficially represented by George of Ostia and the abbot Wigbod) betray some parallelism of English and Frankish interests in Church reform; in particular, recent Carolingian creations of archbishoprics find an echo in the creation of the Mercian archbishopric of Lichfield. Alcuin, too, was present with up-to-date information on such matters. Ecgfrith was anointed king either by the new archbishop or by the legates; he was thus associated in his father's rule, 'à la carolingienne'. Mr. John claims for this anointing an insular background.[69] He points to possible Celtic and even Northumbrian precedents for the existence of a physical ceremony of royal ordination. I should not be very ready to associate such ordination, which may have been no more than a ritual blessing or laying-on of hands, with the anointings devised by Rome to make the

---

[66] See F. Dölger, 'Die "Familie der Könige" im Mittelalter', *Byzanz und die europäische Staatenwelt*, pp. 34–69. I am indebted to the discussion of royal unction in Dr. Janet Nelson's unpublished Cambridge Ph.D. thesis, 'Rituals of royal inauguration in early medieval Europe: from Dux Populi to Athleta Christi'.

[67] *Ann. Regn. Fr.*, s.a. 781.

[68] *Codex Carolinus*, no. 92; *MGH Epist.* iii *Mero. et Karo Aevi*, i), p. 629. Cf. Stenton, *Anglo-Saxon England*, pp. 213 ff .

[69] *Orbis Britanniae*, pp. 28–35.

Carolingians kings, or to assume that Roman legates would have taken their model from Northumbria rather than Rome. *Ordinatio* is an uncertain word. What are we to make of the twelfth chapter ('de ordinatione et honore regum') of the legatine report of 787?[70] Should we allow a technical meaning to its phrase 'sic nec Christus Domini esse valet, et rex totius regni et haeres patriae, qui ex legitimo non fuerit connubio generatus'? It may be that we should, though I am sceptical.[71] In any event, Mr. John is on firm ground in connecting this thought of the legates not primarily with Offa but with his Northumbrian contemporaries,[72] though perhaps they had both in mind. The Northumbrian penchant for royal assassination may well have distressed them. On the other hand, legitimacy was a big consideration for Offa and Ecgfrith.

It also reminds us that Charlemagne's interest in England was not confined to Offa; had it been so, Offa might have been more comfortable in his mind. It involved other kings. First, we may look at the abortive marriage negotiations between the two kings that resulted in a temporary trade embargo. Charlemagne wished his eldest son, Charles, to marry one of Offa's daughters.[73] Offa would only agree if his own son, Ecgfrith, were given Charlemagne's daughter Bertha in marriage. Charlemagne, 'aliquantulum commotus', broke off the negotiation. Why? He may have thought himself demeaned; or again, he may, as Einhard said, have wished to keep all his daughters at home. It seems to me likelier that he sensed a certain distrust in Offa's request, as if Offa planned to keep a Carolingian hostage at his court; for the background to such marriage-negotiations was as often an attempt to patch up bad relations as to give effect to already good ones. Charlemagne, after all, could have used a Mercian princess at his court to influence Offa's enemies in England or Francia;

[70] Haddan and Stubbs, iii, p. 453. The Carolingians speak of *unction*: e.g. in the *arenga* of Pippin III's charter of 762 for Prüm—'quia divina nobis providentia in solium regni unxisse manifestum est' (*MGH Dipl. Karo.*, p. 22, no. 16).

[71] Even Hincmar, who attached great importance to royal unction, explained that kings were called *christi Domini* after Christ: 'a cujus nominis derivatione christi Domini appellantur' ('De divortio Lotharii et Tetbegae', *Pat. Lat.* cxxv, col. 700a, b).

[72] *Orbis Britanniae*, p. 34.

[73] Lohier and Laporte, *Gesta S.P. Font.*, ch. 2, pp. 86 ff.

and these certainly existed.[74] The projected marriage, and still more the atmosphere it engendered, may be the basis of two later tales linking Charlemagne and Offa in marriage: that of Drida in the thirteenth-century St. Albans *Vitae Duorum Offarum*,[75] and a tale reported by Asser that Offa's daughter Eadburh fled to Charlemagne after the death of her husband, Beorhtric of Wessex.[76] The wrappings of the second story are legendary but the contents may not be so. Furthermore, Egbert of Wessex was received in Francia when driven out by Offa in 789,[77] and remained there for at least three years.[78] He returned to Wessex in 802, after Offa's death, perhaps with Frankish help; perhaps, too, none the worse for lessons learnt at the Carolingian court.[79] In general, Offa was sensitive to the presence of Englishmen in Francia, and once even doubted Alcuin's loyalty.[80] There was no knowing how far Charlemagne's *munificentia* might reach. For example, he made gifts to English churches and kings from his Avar treasure-hoard captured in 795. This was to be in return for prayers for his royal *stabilitas* and the extension of Christianity under him:[81] 'fideliter peragite que deposcit.' *Reges Scotorum*, now or on some other occasion, were his pensioners.[82] Offa got some Avar wargear and was requested to pray for Charlemagne, his faithful people, and the whole *populus christianus*.[83] King Æthelred of Northumbria would also have had a share if he had not been murdered. This murder roused Charlemagne to a notable display of anger; Alcuin told Offa that he had almost decided to intervene against

[74] Compare the situation created by the many Lombard refugees in Francia, and Frankish refugees in Lombard territory, before Charlemagne's first journey to Italy: Carlrichard Brühl, *Fodrum, Gistum, Servitium Regis* (Cologne, 1968), i, p. 396.

[75] Ed. R. W. Chambers, *Beowulf, an Introduction to the Study of the Poem* (2nd ed., 1932), pp. 217–43. See, however, K. Sisam, *The Structure of Beowulf* (1965), appendix.

[76] *Asser's Life of King Alfred* (1904), ed. W. H. Stevenson, chs. 14, 15, pp. 12 ff.

[77] See Stevenson, ibid., p. 207.

[78] See Stenton, *Anglo-Saxon England*, p. 218, n. 4; Levison, *England and the Continent*, p. 113.

[79] As conjectured by Levison, ibid., p. 113.

[80] *MGH Epist.* iv, *Karo. Aevi*, ii, p. 125, no. 82; also p. 128, no. 85 and p. 145, no. 100.

[81] Ibid., pp. 150 ff., no. 104.

[82] Cf. *Vita Karoli Magni*, p. 16, ch. 16.

[83] *MGH Epist.* iv, *Karo. Aevi*, ii, p. 146, no. 100.

those who had shown perfidy to their king.[84] Alcuin himself was horrified by the shedding of royal blood. It was not a threat to Offa but it did show that Charlemagne's view of his duty to the *populus christianus* could embrace kingdoms outside his immediate political control. After Offa's death Charlemagne gave a still clearer indication of this by restoring King Eardwulf to Northumbria. Eardwulf may have been married to a Carolingian princess if the Lindisfarne annals can bear that interpretation.[85] At all events, he took refuge in Francia in 808, and in 809 was restored by Charlemagne and the pope, acting jointly: 'per legatos Romani pontificis et domni imperatoris in regnum suum reducitur', says the royal annalist.[86] Eardwulf, himself an anointed king, was the *fidelis* of an emperor who exercised *imperialis defensio*. With Eardwulf thus restored to Northumbria and Egbert, a Carolingian protégé, back in Wessex, King Cenwulf of Mercia (also an anointed king) may well have watched his step. Certainly he mistrusted the next emperor, whom he referred to as 'Caesar'.[87] In brief, Charlemagne looked formidable to his English contemporaries, especially those willing to experiment with the magic of unction; and, further, they knew that he interpreted his special Christian authority, royal or imperial, as sufficient to justify intervention in the affairs of others.[88]

I return to Alcuin in his English context. There survive several of his letters to English kings and others where he teaches them lessons in kingship already familiar to the Carolingians; indeed, he does so in much the same language,[89] as might have been expected. This is not to say that he considered their tasks identical because their virtues should be. An independent king like Offa plainly ruled over a *populus Dei*;[90] in this sense there were

[84] Ibid., pp. 147 ff., no. 101.
[85] Ed. Levison, *Deutsches Archiv*, xvii (1961), pp. 447–506, 483.
[86] *Ann. Regni Fr.*, s.a. 808, pp. 126 ff.
[87] Haddan and Stubbs, iii, p. 587. For Cenwulf's unction see Birch, *Cart. Sax.* i, p. 509, no. 370.
[88] For his relations with the Asturian and Beneventan Churches see H. Löwe, 'Von den Grenzen des Kaisergedankens in der Karolingerzeit', *Deutsches Archiv*, xiv (1958), pp. 354 ff.
[89] The point is made by L. Wallach, *Alcuin and Charlemagne*, p. 62.
[90] *MGH Epist.* iv, *Karo. Aevi*, ii, pp. 147 ff., no. 101 (to Offa in 796); p. 181, no. 123 (to Cenwulf in 797).

many *populi christiani* with kings of their own. But as time
passed it became clear to Alcuin that because of God's special
dispensation Charlemagne was the supreme leader of all;[91] he
had a moral overseership which, as we have seen, he recognized
and might be induced to implement against opposition. In letters
to Æthelred and Eardwulf of Northumbria and to Offa, Ecgfrith
and Cenwulf of Mercia, Alcuin preaches the well-established
kingly virtues; mostly notably, in a letter to Eardwulf in 796:[92]
the king must cultivate the moral virtues and orthodoxy if he
is to enforce them upon his people; and he must listen to the
bishops. For their part, bishops must never be afraid of preach-
ing to kings. Altogether, the pursuit of virtue is conceived very
much as a military operation. It is a reminder that the reforming
synods of Offa's time were a major event in the history of kingship as well as of the Church, in England as on the continent.
The passion for orthodoxy was not Charlemagne's alone. The
English kings, too, were made to feel that they were leaders of
a new Church, and a Church endangered. It has been argued that
the presence of English representatives at Charlemagne's great
reforming synod of Frankfurt in 794[93] is a myth; and an unnecessary myth, since its main business, the heresy of Adoptionism, did not affect England; and further, that Charlemagne's
own witness that such representatives were present was merely
Alcuin's roundabout way of saying that he personally was there.[94]
The words, however, are explicit and, if written by Alcuin, were
written in his master's name. Apart from Adoptionism the
synod discussed monastic discipline, episcopal and metropolitical
jurisdiction, and other matters of interest to the English Church.
Nothing seems to me to be likelier than that English representatives were at Frankfurt.

Alcuin's letters also betray a little of what Scandinavian raids
were beginning to mean for kings. The years 792 and 793 were
critical for England as for Francia. There was famine, associated

[91] Cf. Anton, *Fürstenspiegel*, p. 121. This is clear before the imperial coronation.

[92] *MGH Epist.* iv, *Karo. Aevi*, ii, p. 155, no. 108.

[93] Cf. Charlemagne's letter to Elipand, *MGH Conc. Aevi Karo.*, I. i, p. 159:
'necnon et de Brittanniae partibus aliquos ecclesiasticae disciplinae viros
convocavimus.'

[94] Wallach, *Alcuin and Charlemagne*, p. 166.

with portents; there was the sack of Lindisfarne and, abroad, the revolt of the Saxons. The Anglo-Saxon chronicler is as anxious as the fathers assembled at Frankfurt. In Alcuin's mind it stirred recollections of his countrymen's past, their pagan beginnings and their prosperity under Christian rule.[95] In England as abroad it seemed like a divine judgement on national shortcomings of a moral kind; to appease God was the first step towards successful military resistance. Influenced by disaster, the Northumbrian annalist looked wistfully at Charlemagne's imperial coronation, which the king had accepted, he thought, 'ut imperator totius orbis appellaretur et esset'.[96] Alcuin wrote three letters to King Æthelred of Northumbria, the first immediately after the sack of Lindisfarne.[97] 'Numquam talis terror prius apparuit in Brittannia', he begins. St. Cuthbert's Lindisfarne, 'locus cunctis in Brittannia venerabilior', has fallen to the *pagani*. 'Quis hoc quasi captam patriam non plangit?' What has been the cause of this? Fornication, adultery, incest, avarice, rapine, and injustice, since the days of King Ælfwald. 'Pro huiusmodi peccatis reges regna et populos patriam perdidisse.' Moreover, there had been plenty of warning portents, all symptomatic of the moral disintegration of Northumbrian kingship and society. What is to be done about it? Instant moral reform; the time is ripe for *correctio* and *emendatio*. In the same year Alcuin again addresses Æthelred, but at greater length, on the subject of royal virtues,[98] which he associates closely with the good or ill fortune of his people; and later on he writes a third time,[99] reinforcing his views by a letter to the Mercian Ecgfrith.[100] In both of these he lays some stress on the charisma of royal blood and the significance of belonging to a *gens regia*: it should heighten a king's desire to pursue kingly virtue; the young Ecgfrith will not forget that he is

---

[95] *MGH Epist.*, iv, *Karo. Aevi*, ii, p. 58, no. 20.

[96] Symeon of Durham, ii, *Hist. Regum*, s.a. 800, p. 64. H. Löwe, *Deutsches Archiv*, xiv, p. 352, is not necessarily right to suppose that the annalist's account of the coronation reflects more the outlook of the exiled English than of the English at home. R. Pauli, 'Karl der Grosse in northumbrischen Annalen', *Forschungen zur deutschen Geschichte*, xii (1872), p. 164, reasonably infers some basis in fact for the annalist's account of the years 799–800.

[97] *MGH Epist.* iv, *Karo. Aevi*, ii, pp. 42 ff., no. 16.

[98] Ibid., pp. 49 ff., no. 18.

[99] Ibid., p. 72, no. 30.

[100] Ibid., p. 105, no. 61.

'nobilissimus natus', his father's pupil in *auctoritas*, his mother's in *pietas*. To Offa twice,[101] to Eardwulf once,[102] and to Cenwulf once,[103] he writes in the same vein, to associate the king's actions with his people's prosperity. Alcuin's is not the language of mild moral exhortation to good kings in sunny days; it is the language of urgent reproof generated by insecurity and disaster. Offa, notably, was a king who spent much of his time fighting to establish his hold over central England and to hand on what he had won to his heir; he was more like Clovis than Charlemagne; and, like Clovis, acted with a ruthlessness derived from a sense of insecurity. He would not have ignored Alcuin's opinions, any more than Charlemagne did.[104] If we need any assurance of the seriousness of *correctio* in his eyes, we need only turn to the legate George of Ostia's report to the pope on the legatine council in the south of England; there, he says, the chapters were read out clearly to Offa and his followers 'tam Latine quam theodiscae'.[105] Offa, like Charlemagne, saw the use of vernacular; he wanted to understand what it was he was committing himself to, what it was that he and others had to do.

With this thought-world, where Offa moved with Charlemagne, it seems natural to associate the greatest of all Germanic vernacular epics, *Beowulf*; more natural than to associate it with an earlier time (the age of Bede). I speak without knowledge here, being no linguist, but the arguments that weigh with me are, rather, historical. Professor Whitelock has made a reasoned case for placing the poem in the later eighth century (while not excluding an earlier date) and considers it 'a possible and an attractive hypothesis' that it originated at the court of Offa.[106] One reason for doing so is the little episode of Thryth, perhaps inserted at a later stage by the poet or someone else; for Thryth is here the wife of Offa of Angel, and for him the poet reserves his warmest praise: he is 'the best of men, they say, the wide world over. So Offa ruled his own land wisely and, as befits a brave

[101] *MGH Epist.* iv, *Karo. Aevi*, ii, p. 107, no. 64; p. 147, no. 101.
[102] Ibid., p. 155, no. 108.
[103] Ibid., p. 180, no. 123. See Anton, *Fürstenspiegel*, pp. 90 ff.
[104] Alcuin expected Offa to read his letter (*MGH Epist* iv, *Karo. Aevi*, ii, p. 106, no. 62).
[105] Ibid., p. 28, no. 3.
[106] *The Audience of Beowulf* (1958), p. 64.

warrior, was famous for his victories and gifts.'[107] Dr. Sisam, also
attracted by this, makes the further point that the episode ends
with the names of three members of the Mercian royal house.[108]
It is difficult not to see here a deliberate tribute to the forebears
of the Mercian Offa, such as he would have liked to hear. When
we turn to consider the kind of kingship that *Beowulf* portrays
(and there is a good deal of it) it seems still more likely that the
poet wrote during or soon after Offa's reign and not earlier. I am
supposing that *Beowulf* was intended for a court audience; an
audience, I mean, of warriors primarily, though there is nothing
in it to worry a court cleric. The poem, indeed, presupposes
hearers who would understand at least some biblical allusions
and some Christian dogma,[109] but from this I would not adduce a
monastic audience,[110] to whom such a poem would have been an
irrelevance too huge for even the most lenient of abbots to overlook. It is not at all the same matter as shorter pieces about Ingeld,
Finnsburh, and the like. It is 'literature for entertainment' on a
grand scale, conceived in a way to hold the attention of men who
relished the technicalities of treasure-giving, fighting, courtly
etiquette, and the relationship of lords with their followers.[111]

What, then, was the poet's idea of a good king? Up to a point,
the answer has already been provided in a few pages by Professor Schücking,[112] and his conclusions can be summarized thus:
Beowulf is himself the embodiment of the Christian kingly
virtues and at the same time of those traditional pagan kingly
virtues that were compatible with Christianity. He was the *rex
justus*: wise, pious, kind and humble, careful of and considerate
for those he ruled; the dragon-slayer is in effect the Good Shep-
herd who perishes in protecting his flock. Dying, he is full of pride
and thankfulness for what he has been able to do for his people;
he looks back on his career as one of loyalty and faithfulness:

[107] *Beowulf*, ed. F. Klaeber (3rd ed., 1922), lines 1955–9. I am indebted to my
wife for this translation, as also for expert help with *Beowulf*.
[108] *The Structure of Beowulf*, p. 50.
[109] As Professor Whitelock argues, *Audience of Beowulf*, pp. 5, 6.
[110] As does Professor A. Campbell, 'The Old English epic style', *English and
Medieval Studies Presented to J. R. R. Tolkien* (1962), pp. 13–15.
[111] Sisam notes this, *Structure of Boewulf*, pp. 10 ff.
[112] Levin L. Schücking, 'Das Königsideal im Beowulf', *MHRA Bulletin*, iii
(1929), pp. 143–54. I cite the translation of this article in *An Anthology of
Beowulf Criticism*, ed. Lewis E. Nicholson (Notre Dame, 1963), pp. 35–49.

no enemy has dared to attack his kingdom, he has committed no bad deeds, broken no oath, perpetrated no wrong against his relatives; he has acquired precious possessions for his people. Hrothgar, too, is a good king: peaceful, benevolent, fatherly, quick to accept divine decisions obediently, the enemy of pride. The poet emphasizes the intellectual and moral qualities proper to a ruler: he must be wise, prudent, a good speaker—in effect, a good teacher;[113] he will care for his warriors and be friendly to them, benevolent and warm-hearted, self-renouncing and modest, humble about his triumphs, magnanimous to his enemies, welcoming to strangers, a pious prince of peace—as he is, indeed, in other Germanic epics.[114] In a word, Beowulfian kingship is no exhibition of blind, unbridled courage and fierce wrath, but something much nearer the ideal of Augustine, Gregory the Great, Pseudo-Cyprian, and Isidore. The poet cannot, of course, fill out his picture with specific references to Christianity; he cannot make Beowulf long for the rewards of heaven; for he knows, and his audience knows, that the world of Beowulf was pagan. One should no more expect a reference to Christ in *Beowulf* than a Bible at Sutton Hoo. Schücking concludes that Beowulf 'is the first example of a design of a personality turned towards the "sobrietas" or "mensura" ideal'.[115] And he is a royal personality. It seems to me that we are not here faced, as Schücking believed,[116] with a vernacular mirror of princes for a young ruler. The poet is rather reassuring his king that the virtues he was familiar with were also practised in an earlier time by his pagan ancestors: in brief, that he need not be ashamed of them but rather take courage from their example. The royal Christian virtues are not so new; they need not be objects of suspicion; for they are pretty well those that brought

---

[113] Schücking draws attention (p. 42) to a comparable passage in the *Wanderer* (38), where the deserted vassal yearns to return to his king's 'teaching'.

[114] For example Professor Campbell, 'Old English epic style', p. 15, draws attention to the diffusion of manuscripts of *Waltharius* in continental monasteries. The Old Saxon *Heliand*, composed soon after Charlemagne's death, is the reverse aspect of monastic interest in epic, for here heroic matter is incapsulated in the story of Christ and not, as in *Beowulf*, Christian virtues in heroic material. It is also worth observing how closely the Beowulfian royal virtues are paralleled by the list given by Smaragdus.

[115] Op. cit., p. 46.

[116] Ibid., p. 36.

fame to his house in the old days. This is not to say that the poet was necessarily unfamiliar with mirrors of princes. Indeed, what one might call his specular approach suggests that he could have read not merely Pseudo-Cyprian but some of the more up-to-date hortatory letters, such as St. Boniface and Alcuin wrote to kings. We are more in the age of Alcuin than of Bede. And this, combined with the poet's praise of the continental Offa and his house, would incline me quite strongly towards the court of the Mercian Offa or his son Ecgfrith as the likeliest home for the *Beowulf* poet. It may also not be irrelevant to the situation of Offa and Ecgfrith that the poem envisages joint kingship in situations where a king needed a junior partner designated to succeed him or a minor needed a protector.[117] Let the poet be a cleric; it is a reasonable assumption; and let there be clerics at court and elsewhere to enjoy what Einhard calls the recorded 'barbara et antiquissima carmina, quibus veterum regum actus et bella canebantur'.[118] It only serves to emphasize the close cultural interests of court and Church in the eighth century and the background of harmony against which churchmen were able to present their particular view of a king's function.

Knowing as we do the frequent exchanges between England and the continent in the eighth century, the temptation must always be strong to detect direct influence of one upon the other. Except when the evidence is irrefutable, the temptation should be resisted. In the matter of kingship, we have seen how the same writings were available to form a background to thought on either side of the Channel. We have seen also that mounting military pressures, the nearness of paganism, and the building-up of great overlordships in circumstances more hazardous than they may now look, were equally a common background. Against such, ideas of kingship were to draw even closer together in the ninth century.

[117] *Beowulf*, lines 2369–79. On the death of Hygelac, his widow Hygd offers the throne to Beowulf, who refuses it but stands by to help until the young heir is old enough to rule alone. On his death, Beowulf succeeds him. Klaeber, pp. xxxi–xxxiii, thinks that the case of Hrothgar and his nephew Hrothulf is an example of dual kingship: they sat together in the hall. This is not necessarily so.

[118] *Vita Karoli Magni*, ch. 29 (ed. Holder-Egger, p. 29).

VI

CHARLES THE BALD AND ALFRED

I STARTED these lectures on kingship in the time of the Germanic invasion of the Later Empire and have followed it through times not much less disturbed. And so I come to kingship in the midst of yet another invasion, that of the Vikings, of whom I will say just this: it is possible to cut the Vikings down to size by emphasizing the smallness of their numbers, the limitations of what they could do, and the special interest of clerical writers in stressing their destructiveness.[1] Yet it seems that the sufferers were not only churches and monasteries; others, too, faced disruption, the sense of insecurity of possessions of all kinds, and the disintegration of loyalties. The moral as well as the physical threat bit deep into Frankish and English life; and in an age obsessed with the social problem of sin, it followed that the Vikings would look very like divine judgement on peoples that had lost direction. Revolt or disloyalty of any kind suggested the same conclusion. Thus it struck King Alfred, and thus, too, a generation earlier, Charlemagne's successor, the Emperor Louis the Pious. As we should expect, Louis's reforming friends encouraged this belief. But he was a man who could see for himself that the Christian unity he believed he had inherited stood up ill to the strains of family ambition. So he looked for reconciliation and peace through confession of moral failure and penance; as at Attigny in 822,[2] when it seemed to him that a general penance that included himself as king strengthened his kingship; indeed, it caused him to be compared with Theodosius, a penitent emperor numbered among the Christian heroes.[3] Again, at Soissons in 833, he accepted a yet greater penance for his moral shortcomings; one that temporarily deprived him of

[1] Such is the approach of P. H. Sawyer, *The Age of the Vikings* (1962).
[2] Cf. L. Halphen, *Charlemagne et l'empire carolingien* (Paris, 1947), pp. 247 ff.
[3] Astronomer, *Vita Hludowici*, ed. R. Rau, p. 314, ch. 35.

rule.[4] Perhaps it did not damage the authority of kingship for a king voluntarily to resign, as he did, in favour of an already-appointed successor, as much as its outcome damaged the credibility of the Frankish bishops as exponents of kingship. What did damage kingship, and what did cause an indignant reaction in his favour, was his humiliating treatment at his son's hands; and so he was restored, 'divina repropitiante clementia',[5] to his kingship and empire. However, a point had been made in a clumsy fashion: royal power could only be exercised rightly: to exercise it wrongly was a negation of that power that implied self-deprivation. This was remembered by Louis's youngest son and successor, Charles the Bald; and it occurred also to Alfred, as he revealed in his translation of Boethius. We may notice another feature of the crisis of the Emperor Louis's reign. If David and Solomon could be paraded as exemplars for good rulers, Ahab, Manasseh, Jezebel, and others were equally valid warnings of the fate of bad rulers; and they were more than warnings. If the Franks really were the New Israel and the Bible their final court of appeal, it followed that bad rulers of the Old Testament were to be seen historically as the lineal predecessors of the Carolingians: what could happen in the Old Israel could equally happen in its successor, the New Israel. Surely this, rather than unction, is what fostered the suspicion of the ninth century that bad kings were dispensable?[6]

Not all the disruption of ninth-century life can be attributed to the Vikings; ancient regional loyalties could look very like disloyalty to a hard-pressed king, especially when it meant his subjects treating with his enemies; and it was only to be expected that churches and monasteries would feel a special need in unsettled times to reorganize the defence of their property and claim back, if they could, some of the wealth that earlier reforming Carolingians had confiscated. To many churchmen it seemed obvious what the role of their king should be: to restore, to protect, and not to interfere. The terms of the treaty of Coulaines

[4] Halphen, *Charlemagne*, p. 293.
[5] B. Simson, *Jahrbücher des fränkischen Reichs unter Ludwig dem Frommen* (Leipzig, 1874–6), ii, pp. 90–2.
[6] The polemical writings of the crisis are considered by Egon Boshof, *Erzbischof Agobard von Lyon* (Cologne, 1969).

in 843 are a clear statement of their position.[7] It is also exemplified in the famous dispute between the monastery of St. Calais and the bishopric of Le Mans in 863; the only escape from their bishop, as the threatened monastery found, was into the arms of the king—and this after a royal investigation ordered not by the king but by Pope Nicholas I.[8] Royal *defensio* was a duty that cannot often have looked attractive to kings; yet they sought to carry it out, amidst a welter of forged charters and bitter reminders that they must not exceed their duty. The matter of property is thus basic to the thinking of ninth-century churchmen about royal power: the king was to be busy in charter-interpretation, litigation, and the general supervision of claims and counter-claims deriving from secular gifts, and in the use of armed power when necessary. It was a duty that could often merge into the other duty of royal defence against external aggressors, especially in a rich and exposed province like Reims. If to a large extent the Church made kingship, it was kingship that saved the Church.[9] Defence of church-property was made none the easier in a situation where royal property was itself being whittled away by constant alienation through donations. There was contemporary disquiet at this, at least in the reign of Louis the Pious.[10] Charles the Bald, in particular, whose position as a landowner was weaker than Alfred's in England, found that he had too little land available to satisfy the Church, let alone buy the loyalty of magnates who were attracted by offers from kings who were his competitors.[11] His *acta*[12] bear all too much evidence of the extent to

[7] Cf. F. Lot and L. Halphen, *Le Règne de Charles le Chauve*, i (Paris, 1909), p. 91.

[8] See the exhaustive treatment of the incident by Walter Goffart, *The Le Mans forgeries* (Cambridge, Mass., 1966); for Charles the Bald's general attitude to ecclesiastical property, see E. Lesne, *Histoire de la propriété ecclésiastique en France*, ii, 2, and Carlrichard Brühl, *Fodrum, Gistum, Servitium Regis*, ch. 1.

[9] Hincmar may have saved Charles the Bald, but that is another matter. See, for example, the recent view of Walter Schlesinger, 'Die Auflösung des Karlsreiches', *Karl der Grosse*, i, p. 841.

[10] J. Dhondt, *Études sur la naissance des principautés territoriales en France* (Bruges, 1948), p. 13 and *passim*.

[11] Brühl, op. cit., p. 50, contends that Charles's large alienations to buy the support of magnates caused him to lean much more heavily on the Church and its property than his predecessors had done.

[12] *Recueil des actes de Charles II le Chauve*, 3 vols. (Paris, 1943–55), ed. A. Giry, M. Prou, and G. Tessier.

which he had to despoil his own domains to buy off revolt and
foreign attack; Archbishop Hincmar, for example, forced him
to restore all benefices granted away from the Church of Reims.[13]
His resources in land were nothing like those of his grandfather,
Charlemagne; yet he was a powerful king, not always ready to
alienate without a struggle; and his position in relation to his
magnates was infinitely stronger than was that of his successors:[14] in relation also to his bishops, of whom the formidable
Hincmar was not entirely typical.[15] Even so, his unprecedented
and unwelcome reliance on bishops and abbots for hospitality
and the upkeep of his court was bound in the long run to play
into their hands.[16] Of his legislative and corrective authority he
had no doubt; and this he made abundantly plain to Pope
Hadrian, when he informed him by letter that 'I am a king
chosen by God (regem a Deo constitutum) set apart as a two-
edged sword, the punisher of the wicked and defender of
the innocent, so that I can wreak vengeance on evil-doers,
as St. Paul puts it'.[17] He goes on to insist on his legal authority,
which embraces bishops, too. The words may be those of
the archbishop of Reims, but the thoughts are authentically
the king's. A king, as Samuel knew when he honoured Saul,
was always a man to whom reverence was due. 'Read the
Book of Kings', Hincmar advises Louis the German, 'to see
what reverence is due to a brother king.'[18] The Carolingians were
kings whose armed might commanded obedience. Authority,
not piety, is depicted in the portrait of Louis the Pious as a
miles christianus in the copy of Hraban Maur's *De laudibus
sancti crucis* dedicated to the king himself.[19] The background,

[13] See Dhondt, *Études*, p. 29.

[14] For example Louis the Stammerer started his reign with a very large
distribution of honours and abbeys (*Annales Bertiniani*, ed. F. Grat, p. 218,
s.a. 877).

[15] Charles did not hesitate to arraign Bishop Hincmar of Laon in the royal
court for infidelity (Hincmar of Reims, *Schedula*, ch. 10, *Pat. Lat.* cxxvi,
cols. 525 ff.).

[16] Cf. Brühl, *Fodrum, Gistum, Servitium Regis*, p. 50.

[17] *Pat. Lat.* cxxiv, col. 889. Ullmann, *Caro. Ren.*, p. 180, rightly stresses the
influence of Pauline doctrine on the development of the idea of *tuitio*, which
may be loosely defined as 'guardianship' or 'protection'.

[18] *Pat. Lat.* cxxvi, cols. 9–25.

[19] Vienna MS., Öst. Nat. Bibl. Cod. 652, fo. 3ᵛ (an early copy of the original).
The portrait is reproduced in *Karl der Grosse, Werk und Wirkung* (Aaachen,

then, to ninth-century kingship is social disruption seen as God's judgement on sin, with its necessary concomitants of royal *correctio* and penance, royal protection of threatened interests, and royal concern for unity, dynastic and national, sometimes seen as Christian, but more often and more simply as the legacy of Charlemagne.

The cult of Charlemagne, for which there is no parallel in England, marks the true measure of kingship for his successors; a cult, like all cults, rooted in ascertainable fact but flourishing on myth. The ninth-century Charlemagne, however, was very different from the gorgeous figure of the developed medieval cult.[20] Einhard's Charlemagne, conceived in the 820s, is fairly complex; but, whatever he is, he is not a heroic Church-creature.[21] He is a father-figure, happiest in his family circle, and a great national king, thoroughly secular when it came to the point, though pious in intention. The dissemination of manuscripts of Einhard's Life suggests that this was precisely the picture of Charlemagne that a new generation wanted—a new generation that included Charles the Bald personally if, as seems likely, the Leningrad MS. F. IV. 4 of Einhard, written in the scriptorium of St. Médard at Soissons, should be associated with the court.[22] At the end of the century Notker of St. Gallen's *Gesta Karoli Magni*,[23] written for the Emperor Charles the Fat, are a new interpretation of Einhard's Charlemagne, and an act of monastic appropriation. The Charlemagne of the *Gesta* is the idealized Christian ruler, a Davidic figure rather as Alcuin had seen him; and at the same time he is the idealized iron warrior, whose deeds of war ought to be better known than they are. Notker plumps for a selection of muddled anecdotes that leave a strong

---

1965), opposite p. 304; the manuscript is described in the same catalogue, p. 307, no. 497.

[20] On which see *Karl der Grosse*, iv: *Das Nachleben*.

[21] The point emerges clearly from Folz, *Le Souvenir*, bk. 1.

[22] Note the singular title, which suggests a royal dedication: 'Vita et conversatio gloriosissimi imperatoris Karoli atque invictissimi augusti incipit edita ab Eginardo sui temporis impense doctissimo necnon liberalium experientissimo artium viro, educato a prefato principe, propagatore et defensore religionis Christianae, quam *feliciter perlegendo currentes laetimini in Christo*' (my italics). I owe this information to Professor Bernhard Bischoff.

[23] Ed. H. F. Haefele, *MGH Script. Rer. Germ.*, n.s. xii (Berlin, 1959).

impression of royal virtue: deeds of courage, cunning, wisdom, restraint, piety, and generosity; these are what the latest Charles needed to hear about. His family is presented to him with all the right gifts for rule; they have them by heredity as much as by God's gift and the best of them had not been dominated by bishops or popes. Even so, the *Gesta* were a private and local interpretation, not destined for wide circulation before the twelfth century. Meanwhile, others constructed their own Charlemagnes in the way most useful to them. Already in the ninth century he is the victim of forged diplomas, a desirable addition to local genealogies and necrologies, and the king whom the authors of Saints' Lives could reasonably link with the extension of Christianity. Few were much concerned with the juridical fact of his having been an emperor as well as a king. It mattered more that he had ruled several Germanic kingdoms as a great Christian warrior: his *nomen* corresponded with his achievement. So he appeared to his ninth-century successors.

Charlemagne's preoccupation with learning descended to his successors. Learned kings, or at least kings who were patrons of learning, are therefore the rule and not the exception in the ninth century. Louis the Pious certainly did not share all his father's literary interests; he loved the radical Church-reformers too well for that. In consequence, the Council of Paris in 829 saw fit to remind him of his duty to protect learning,[24] which, in the opinion of some, including Servatus Lupus, was not what it had once been.[25] Yet he appointed the great Walahfrid as his son's tutor, and at least two centres of learning (St. Denis and Corbie) had reason to be grateful to him. Circumstances seem to have been against him in this, as in much else. At the beginning of the first and happiest decade of his reign he could be acclaimed as a new David and a new Solomon,[26] on whom men could centre their hopes of unity; the epithet *pius* as applied to him was one of aspiration.[27] Aachen was still the imperial home of learning, and so remained till 843. There, under royal protection, the continuation of the *Annales Regni Francorum*, later known

---

[24] *MGH Conc.* ii. 2, p. 675.
[25] *Correspondance*, ed. L. Levillain, i (Paris, 1927), p. 4, letter 1.
[26] *Pat. Lat.* cv, col. 988.
[27] So Ewig, *Das Königtum*, p. 70.

as the St. Bertin Annals, were composed in what has been called a 'bureau historique'.[28] In the next reign, Prudentius continued these annals on the personal order of Charles the Bald; indeed, the king had his own copy. Royal interest in an official record was hardly surprising: Charles was no sooner king than he ordered Nithard to write the history of his reign.[29] Only when Hincmar became the annalist did the record cease to be official; and we do not know what Charles thought of that. It was the abbey of St. Denis, though not yet as a historiographical centre, that seemed most to attract the Emperor Louis. Such was the power of its learned abbot, his friend and arch-chancellor, Hilduin, that he has even been called, rather wildly, the French vice-pope.[30] Something of what Hilduin thought of kingship may be gleaned from the illustrations to the famous Stuttgart Psalter if the book was written, as it probably was, at St. Germain-des-Prés during the time when Hilduin was abbot there as well as at St. Denis.[31] The David of the Psalter is no Arcadian shepherd-boy. He is much more the David of the Book of Kings (a copy of which, indeed, may have been one of the illustrator's models). The scenes that are chosen for illustration are mostly scenes of bloodshed, war, hand-to-hand combat, hunting, and judgement. Through them David moves as an armed king protected by the massive hand of God; not only protected, but anointed and crowned by the same hand, with Samuel in a supporting role.[32] Christ, when he is depicted, is much the same sort of warrior-king. One cannot indeed always be sure which is Christ and which David. There could be no more forcible reminder of the ninth century's identification of the two, and of both with the work of kingship; and the reminder comes from a Parisian monastery in close touch with the Emperor Louis and presided over by his arch-chancellor.

<hr />

[28] L. Levillain, intro. to F. Grat's ed., p. xii.

[29] *Histoire des fils de Louis le Pieux*, ed P. Lauer (Paris, 1926), prol., pp. 2, 3.

[30] M. Buchner, *Das Vizepapsttum des Abtes von St. Denis* (Paderborn, 1928); see Levison's critical review, reprinted in *Aus rheinischer und fränkischer Frühzeit*, pp. 517–29.

[31] Now Stuttgart, Württembergische Landesbibliothek, Bibl. fol. 23. Described in *Karl der Grosse*, catalogue, p. 303, no. 490. Facsimile text, *Der Stuttgarter Bilderpsalter*, 2 vols. (Stuttgart, 1965).

[32] Fos. 24ʳ, 24ᵛ, 104ʳ.

The Stuttgart Psalter could not suggest that the Christ-like King David was the instrument of a Church; but David's ninth-century successors had their work cut out not to become so. In 877 Pope John VIII hailed Charles the Bald as the *principem populi* established by God in imitation of Christ, the true king; what Christ possessed by nature Charles could have by grace; he was the *salvator mundi*.[33] Anyone could see that there were strings attached to this. Who but the Church was to interpret Christ's kingship in such a situation as the imperial vacancy of 875 when, according to John VIII's formula, Christ himself temporarily assumed direct rule ('regnante imperatore domno Iesu Christo')?[34] We cannot tell how Charles as emperor would have reacted to such language, since he died so soon after becoming emperor; but in his own Frankish kingdom he plainly meant to be master, whatever the implications of Davidic unction or coronation; master, among much else, of the business of *correctio* by way of control of learning. Aachen, the *schola palatina* of his father and grandfather, he lacked; and there was no adequate substitute. Instead, he distributed his favours widely, with a marked preference for St. Denis (his own lay-abbacy, which he personally defended against the Danes),[35] Metz (the home of the cult of his forebear, St. Arnulf),[36] Compiègne or Carlopolis (his own foundation), and Reims (conveniently near his own *palatium* of Quierzy). At all these places there were schools and libraries which benefited from the gifts of (in Lesne's phrase) 'ce roi bibliophile'.[37] None of these exactly corresponded to the Aachen that had been. Heiric of Auxerre insisted that there never was a school in the strict sense at Charles's palace; but he adds that the whole palace seemed to be a kind of school in which all joined: the meeting-place of scholars, magnates, clergy, and promising young men. Hincmar's picture of the *domus regis* bears out

---

[33] Mansi, *Concilia*, xvii, appendix, col. 172.

[34] E. H. Kantorowicz, *The King's Two Bodies* (Princeton, 1957), p. 335.

[35] For a general assessment, see S. M. Crosby, *The Abbey of St. Denis*, i (Yale, 1942), pp. 78 ff.

[36] On the cult of St. Arnulf, and the stress laid on his holiness, see Oexle, 'Die Karolinger und die Stadt des heiligen Arnulf', *Frühmittelalt. Studien*, i (1967), esp. pp. 269 ff.; and, for an important ninth-century genealogy, pp. 252 ff.

[37] *Hist. de la prop. eccl.* iv, *Les Livres*, p. 610.

Heiric's description.[38] Clearly Charles was a better scholar than any of his predecessors, all of whom he surpassed by his 'studium erga immortales disciplinas'. In law particularly he knew what he was doing: 'par Theodosio', remarks a contemporary.[39] His interest in Late Antiquity was markedly stronger than his alleged interest in Byzantium. Philosophers also were attracted to his court, 'ad publicam eruditonem'. He fancied himself as a philosopher-king. John Scotus Eriugena took pupils at court, though whether at Quierzy or nearby at Laon or Reims is not clear.[40] Eriugena was reckoned a court-scholar at any rate, ready to take his part in the theological debates that rocked Francia in the 850s; and a scholar to whom the ninth-century revival of interest in Boethius owed much. If there is any Alfredian book that one would imagine might have come direct from a library in close touch with the Carolingians, it would surely be the *Consolatio Philosophiae*.

In return for his protection of its lands and its learning, Charles expected certain services of the Church. We may note his strong interest in commemorations by the Church of royal anniversaries, after the fashion of the ancient *Natales Caesarum*.[41] Another kind of service is suggested by his picture in the magnificent Bible dedicated to him that is now at San Paolo fuori le mura.[42] It is not the only picture that survives of him but it is the only one that shows him enthroned in the presence of his queen, and probably his second queen, Richildis. The occasion seems to be their marriage; and the presence of the queen (veiled, not crowned) is explained by an inscription expressing the hope that her issue might prove to be distinguished. (As it turned out, she had none.) What the king is expecting of the marriage service is the blessing of heirs more suitable than the children of his

[38] See Heiric's preface to his *Vita S. Germani*, ed. Traube, *MGH Poet.* iii, Hincmar's *De ordine palatii, passim,* and Gottschalk to the same effect in his *Carmen ad Ratramnum, MGH Poet.* iii, p. 736. The best summary is Lesne, *Hist. de la prop. eccl.* v, *Les Écoles,* ch. iii.

[39] *MGH Poet.* iii, p. 243. See Kantorowicz, *Laudes Regiae,* p. 74, n. 31.

[40] Dom Cappuyns, *Jean Scot Érigène* (Brussels, 1964 imp.), pp. 63 ff., leaves the matter open.

[41] Kantorowicz, *Laudes Regiae,* pp. 67, 68, who draws attention to the interest of St. Denis in this matter.

[42] Kantorowicz, 'The Carolingian king in the Bible of San Paolo fuori le mura', *Selected Studies* (New York, 1965), pp. 82–94.

first marriage. The Church is being asked to work a magic, as on other ritual occasions in the reign. The San Paolo Bible is quite possibly a product of the St. Denis scriptorium, to judge from its resemblance to another contemporary manuscript, now in Paris,[43] which contains a picture of the unction of Clovis.[44] Most of all, the element of magic emerges in the royal unctions of Charles's reign.[45] The earlier Carolingians were comparatively unimpressed by anointings.[46] We cannot even tell what significance they attached to clerical participation in their inauguration ceremonies. Louis the Pious did not have his son Charles anointed, despite his weak position. Then the situation changes; unctions become more frequent and more charged with political meaning. They almost look like a belated catching-up on what had been implicit in a century's exposition of Old Testament kingship. In 848 Charles strengthened his hold over Aquitaine

[43] B.N., MS. lat. 1141. Such was the opinion of A. M. Friend. See Kantorowicz, *Selected Studies*, pp. 92–4. We may also notice the presence of a queen in the Stuttgart Psalter, fo. 57v, where David and a queen, both crowned and robed, stand side by side.

[44] This unction was of special interest to Hincmar, once a monk at St. Denis. It was he who first associated the oil used at Clovis's baptism at Reims with royal Frankish unction. Cf. his *Vita Remigii*, ch. 15, *MGH Script, Rer. Mero.* iii, pp. 296–7. I have commented on this in my *Long-Haired Kings*, pp.102 ff.

[45] Much fuller consideration of the significance of unction, especially as seen from the clerical viewpoint, will be found in Ullmann's *Carolingian Renaissance*, notably ch. 4, where a case is made that unction was a vital aspect of the ninth-century concept of the rebirth of society, the ruler being reborn through unction to a specifically Christian role. Ullmann's argument is ideologically sound and is well supported by the clerical sources; it may, however, go too far in dissociating the new society from its historical roots, at least in royal eyes, and take too little account of the political circumstances of each ninth-century anointing. I have the impression that the participation of lay magnates in ceremonies of inauguration was no mere formality to Charles the Bald, notably in Aquitaine and Lotharingia. This impression gains support from Walther Kienast, *Studien über die französischen Volksstämme des Frühmittelalters* (Stuttgart, 1968), pp. 135 ff.

[46] On inauguration ceremonies generally the fundamental studies of P. E. Schramm must be consulted: *Der König von Frankreich* (Weimar, 1960); *Kaiser, Könige und Päpste* (Stuttgart, 1968); *Herrschaftszeichen und Staatssymbolik*, esp. vol. i (Stuttgart, 1954). Reference should also be made to C. A. Bouman, *Sacring and Crowning* (Groningen, 1957) and P. L. Ward, 'The coronation ceremony in mediaeval England', *Speculum*, xiv (1939), pp. 160–78. I have profited much from the unpublished Ph.D. thesis of Dr. Janet Nelson (Cambridge, 1967).

by a ceremony of unction and coronation at Orleans,[47] and again in 858 in Neustria, apparently as a guarantee against the claims of his brother Louis. Two years earlier, at Verberie, his daughter Judith was crowned and anointed by Hincmar as part of her marriage ceremony with the English king, Æthelwulf; and the *ordo* survives. It was done to strengthen her position in England, presumably with the English bishops. Thereafter, ceremonies of unction and coronation proliferate: Lothar II crowned his queens, Waldrada in 862 and Theutberga in 865; Charles's first queen, Irmintrude, was consecrated at Soissons in 866, explicitly with the hope of making her fruitful; at Metz, in 869, Charles himself was crowned and anointed king over Lotharingia; in 875 he was consecrated emperor in Rome by Pope John VIII; and thereafter Louis the Stammerer, Boso (the first non-Carolingian king of the century), and others. The surviving *ordines*, notably Hincmar's, show a growing mastery of the possibilities of this ritual act of inauguration and, inevitably, a dawning realization that the Church could thus control the actions of kings, at least in so far as a king chose to abide by his undertakings at his inauguration and to have his actions reviewed by churchmen in the light of them. How many kings fully grasped the symbolism of the ritual I should not care to guess. As for Charles the Bald, he acknowledged from time to time that his unction gave his consecrators a duty to keep him in the straight path and even to dictate his actions in limited spheres; this was the price of their continued support, and handsomely did the bishops reward him when his brother Louis invaded West Francia. Neither he nor they would have claimed that it gave them any right to depose him; the ancient doctrine still held, that a bad ruler was God's judgement on a sinful people, and as such had better be endured than dispensed with. It remains to determine what importance Charles attached to unction and inauguration ceremonies generally. It must be assumed that he thought they strengthened his kingship. At the lowest level, clergy bound to him in these ceremonies were a

---

[47] Kienast, *Studien*, p. 55, makes the interesting suggestion that the Carolingian genealogies fabricated at Metz, which give Arnulf a Roman senator as grandfather, were an attempt to please or placate the Aquitanian magnates of the ninth century.

safeguard against disaffection and disloyalty in his own kingdom and a support in his ambitions to claim whatever other parts of the empire of Charlemagne he could lay hands on. He may also have felt the force of the argument stated, for example, by the bishops at Pistoia in 862,[48] that he needed the spiritual gifts conferred by consecration to fight the Vikings: it was a means to the military virtues of strength and prudence. Consecration could strengthen the claims of heredity,[49] sanction a usurpation, incline God to make queens fruitful, and bind the clergy to a king they certainly did not choose but presumably thought they made. Charles would have lost nothing by agreeing with Hincmar that unction helped a king to withstand his enemies (visible and invisible), bound him particularly to the task of protecting the Church and its property, and linked him, in the liturgifying way of the time, with the kingship of Christ, the pre-eminently victorious king. I see some, but not much, ecclesiastical ambition in all this. Rather, it looks like the attempt of distracted and threatened churchmen to save what they could by enhancing the power of their king through the only means available to them. The *ordines* are difficult to interpret, but none of them seems to me to 'capture' a king for the Church, in the sense of restraining him in the exercise of his traditional power.

However, these experiments in inauguration were bound to find some echo in the advice tendered to the Carolingians by their clergy; and, from the days of Alcuin, that advice came in a steady stream,[50] of which a mere trickle crossed the Channel to brace the English. It takes the form, mostly, of mirrors of princes, well-rooted in traditional sources. But their tone is not always traditional, and clearly they witness to a growing interest in new problems of kingship. They start with an Aquitanian group, of which the *Via Regia* of the abbot Smaragdus is the earliest example. It is addressed in all probability to Louis the Pious when king of Aquitaine, some time between 811 and 814.[51] What the writer means by his *Via Regia* is the king's way to God,

---

[48] *MGH Capit.* ii, pp. 303 ff.
[49] In his Metz sermon, Hincmar emphasized Charles's hereditary claim as descendant of Clovis and St. Arnulf. Cf. Schramm, *König von Frankreich*, i, p. 27.
[50] It is best summarized by Anton, *Fürstenspiegel*, ch. 3, whom I here follow.
[51] *Pat. Lat.* cii. See Anton, pp. 132–87.

a way that he can best illustrate from the Bible and above all from the career of King David. To all intents and purposes, he sees his king as a kind of abbot—the anointed *vicarius Christi* rather than as the more traditional *vicarius Dei*. What is more, whole passages of the *Via Regia* are repeated by the author in a later work, his *Diadema Monachorum*. In other words, a king's approach to his duties and a monk's (and more specifically an abbot's) are not unlike. Pope Gregory's *Cura Pastoralis* had already suggested that a king's and a bishop's duties had much in common. Smaragdus supplied the king with two versions of the *Via* (prose and verse), and also worked over a Merovingian mirror of princes for one of Louis's sons (probably Pippin of Aquitaine).[52] Soon he found an imitator in Ermoldus Nigellus, the Carolingian historian. Ermold's *In Honorem Hludowici Pii*[53] is a rich mine for regal theory and history; and his two elegies for Pippin of Aquitaine are undisguised mirrors of princes.[54] Well bottomed in Isidore, Ermold preaches the theocratic nature of kingship: he urges his prince to take counsel (especially from the Church), to love his subjects, to be a man, to look after the poor, to be wise, just, and pious, to put down the proud, and not to hunt too much. Only thus might he and his progeny hope for increased power. There are plenty of Old Testament examples to show that only kings who obey God succeed; and Ermold compares his Old Testament heroes with the successful Carolingians, one by one. It is a revealing historical exercise. He ends his more important elegy on a personal note, by wishing Pippin and his wife good luck and victory—and by begging for a little luck on his own account. My inference is this: a Carolingian prince may be expected to be flattered by an address that in effect tells him that his kingship is neither more nor less than a *ministerium* over the secular part of an *imperium christianum*.

If we look at the capitularies and council acts of the ninth century, we shall see that kings took advice of this sort seriously. Louis the Pious, for example, in his *Admonitio*[55]

[52] Anton, p. 186.
[53] Ed. E. Faral, *Ermold le noir* (Paris, 1932).
[54] Ibid. See Anton, pp. 190-8.
[55] *MGH Capit.* i, pp. 303-7, no. 150; Anton, pp. 198-210.

of 823–5, summons the laity and clergy to implement his Christian *ministerium*, the duties of which he enumerates; like Charlemagne, he is a preacher and teacher as well as defender of the Church. The Church's anxiety for its own material independence already appears: it does not want too much defence, and says so. The Paris *acta* of 829[56] are very clear on the distinction between a *rex* and a *tyrannus*: the king must first learn to govern himself, then his house, and finally his people; his *ministerium* consists in ruling God's people with equity and justice so that they may enjoy peace, and this he implements through his power of *correctio* and *defensio*. Nothing more. He is God's king.

A third Aquitanian, Jonas of Orleans, carries the matter a little further in his *De Institutione Regia*,[57] written for Pippin of Aquitaine in 831. It owes more to the Paris *acta* (of which indeed it is a polite résumé) than to Smaragdus. In an Orleans manuscript of some worked-over Aachen *acta*, apparently from the pen of Jonas, occurs a section on the king's duties, military and other. They include a reminder that he should love God more than he loves honour.[58] (King Alfred has something to say on the same matter.) But principally they show Jonas, or his source, facing the problem of the ethics of the just war as it affected kings. In some ways the Aquitanian mirrors of princes were old-fashioned; but they were enough to cause the Carolingians to take a good look at themselves, particularly since they exposed them to the Gelasianism of reforming churchmen.

Belonging to a different milieu we have Servatus Lupus of Ferrières,[59] with his three admonitory letters to Charles the Bald.[60] Humility and piety, says Lupus, must be the precondition of the exercise of power, as David found; only then will the king put down rebellion and make certain of reaching the heavenly kingdom. *Utilitas publica* is the touchstone. The king is reminded of the examples of Trajan and Theodosius. More interesting are the views of Sedulius Scottus, writing

[56] *MGH Conc.* ii, pp. 606–80.
[57] Ed. J. Reviron (Paris, 1930); Anton, pp. 212–44.
[58] Paris, B.N., MS. lat. nouv. acq. 1632; Anton, pp. 221 ff.
[59] See Anton, pp. 248–54.
[60] Ed. L. Levillain, i. no. 31, p. 140; no. 37, p. 160; no. 46, p. 192.

between 840 and 858.[61] His *Liber de Rectoribus Christianis*,[62] intended probably for Lothar II, is more in the tradition of Pseudo-Cyprian and Alcuin than of the Aquitanians. One sees this in his association of royal virtues with the people's luck and in his interpretation of natural phenomena; moreover, *terror*, *amor*, and *ordinatio* are well to the fore. He is strong on the king's *ministerium*, which embraces peace, justice, the protection of the Church, and responsibility for converting the heathen; and there is much on the war-ethics of Moses, Hezekiah, Jehosophat, and Judas Maccabeus. The great exemplars for Sedulius are David, God's servant in destroying *tyranni*, and Solomon, the *rex pacifer*, wise, pious, and temple-building, and, more recently, Constantine and Theodosius the Great. What is a *tyrannus*? It is a king who neglects through *superbia* his Christian duty; also, it is any pagan Dane, and those who support such.[63] In effect, the Carolingians are being asked to be crusaders. The king will bow to the Church in matters of dogma; but Sedulius is not much bothered by Gelasianism.

A greater than Sedulius was Hincmar, for ever reinterpreting the work of kings through a wide range of writings, and always opportunistically with an eye to an urgent problem.[64] Hincmar agreed with Gregory the Great that God had established kingship to deal with the inequality in man brought about by his sin; in this task the king was God's deputy, his *vicarius* as well as his *minister*, and never independent of him. He distinguishes six kinds of ruler, in the making of three of which God actively participates; the remainder He merely permits. Once again, people get the rulers they deserve. Only a king who obeys God's commands is owed obedience; disobedience, however, is not a topic he risks developing. Like Augustine, he sees his Christian king as a warrior, with his people united behind him to attack paganism, within and without. Humility, perhaps of course, is a difficult and over-subtle art for such a ruler, and Hincmar is content to leave it in a secondary place among royal virtues:

---

[61] See Anton, pp. 261–79.

[62] Ed. S. Hellmann, in *Quellen und Untersuchungen zur lateinischen Philologie des Mittelalters*, i. i (Munich, 1906).

[63] *De strage Normannorum, MGH Poet.* iii, pp. 208 ff.

[64] See Anton, pp. 261–79.

justice is more important. The *tyrannus* whom it is proper in theory at least to disobey is the unjust ruler. How will a king prove his justice? By fatherly *correctio*, applied privately within his own family, and publicly; and by *defensio*. Protection against the Danes is never far from Hincmar's mind—understandably, in an archbishop of Reims; anarchy is what he fears. Indeed, this is the burden of his *De Regis Persona*, as well as of several letters. Law must be made and enforced; the poor, the *miser populus*, must be protected, and property also. And to whom is the king answerable for duties thus morally conceived? To God, of course; which means the Church. Except in the matter of Church property and jurisdiction over churchmen, Hincmar keeps clear of Gelasianism; in other words, he sees no practical distinction between Church and State; the king is much more than a secular policeman, though he is that too. When Charles seized Lotharingia, Hincmar was at hand to justify him on the ground of propinquity: men could not obey a far-off king unable to defend them against frequent pagan attacks: they must enjoy freedom 'rectorem eligere qui sanctam ecclesiam . . . defendat et gubernet'.[65] A king so chosen, who did his duty, deserved unswerving obedience. Hincmar was even prepared to turn Gelasius upside down to defend royal power against the papacy; Frankish kings, he told Hadrian II on Charles's behalf, 'non episcoporum vicedomini sed terrae domini hactenus fuimus computati'.[66] Charles was *dominus terrae*; and more, a *rex pius*, the *imago Dei* filled with *gratia*, a king of royal blood.[67] When it came to the *correctio* of kings themselves, then the bishops were to fulfil their time-honoured duty, not only as consecrators but as heirs to the prophets of the Old Testament. One sees the implications of this for the future; but the fact is that Hincmar was not interested in circumscribing royal power, and his colleagues still less. The preoccupation of the Carolingian ecclesiastics with the king's job must be taken at its face value: he alone could save them and the world they knew. His power declines but his authority increases; he is asked to consider himself in the mirror they hold up. By and large he is satisfied with what he sees. No

[65] *Pat. Lat.* cxxvi, col. 176c.
[66] Ibid. cxxiv, cols. 876–81.
[67] Ibid. col. 881c, d.

such mirror of what may be called a technical kind was held up to the English kings; at least, none that we know of. It remains to be asked whether, mirrorless, they took an essentially different view of kingship from that of their Carolingian contemporaries.

The Carolingians at whom I have been looking struggled throughout the ninth century with diminishing success to keep intact Charlemagne's western kingdom and to implement his idea of kingship. Their English contemporaries faced a different situation. The three great West Saxon kings—Egbert, Æthelwulf, and Alfred—were builders rather than heirs; their political situation was more like that of the earlier Carolingians. The record of their reigns makes them look more like their Carolingian contemporaries than they may really have been. This is because we owe that record to the same kind of churchmen, and because, like the Carolingians, they faced the Vikings. Their essential work, however, was the mastering of central England. Mr. John has given a convincing sketch[68] of how Alfred and his father husbanded their patrimony in such a way as not to deprive the crown of its resources in land through division and alienation. The Carolingians had nothing here to teach the West Saxons. With this, Mr. John connects the hallowing of the young Alfred at Rome.[69] Certainly the pope considered himself to be Alfred's spiritual father thereafter, though this does not quite clear up the nature of the ceremony to which Alfred was subjected. At least it is clear that in consequence of his father's foresight and his brothers' comparative restraint he faced the Vikings a richer man than he would otherwise have done. This did not alter the nature of his kingship but it certainly affected its power. It enabled him to fight from an assured background, which was what the Carolingians increasingly lacked.

Alfred's Danish campaigns were more than a military matter. There are plenty of hints that he interpreted them, as the Franks did theirs, in a religious sense; and to this Stenton has given such emphasis as the evidence will bear. The baptism of Guthrum in 878, after his defeat at Edington, was a condition of the arrangement to which he and Alfred had come; and there

[68] *Orbis Britanniae*, pp. 36 ff.

[69] *Anglo-Saxon Chronicle*, s.a. 853; Asser, ed. Stevenson, ch. 8, p. 7. For the pope's letter, see Stevenson, p. 180, n. 1, and *MGH Epist.* iii, p. 602.

was no immediate precedent for this. Abbo of Fleury, not much later, was to see the death of Edmund of the East Anglians in 870 as martyrdom at pagan (that is, Danish) hands. Edmund, he says, stuck to the *via regia*,[70] morally speaking; and the king had an interesting conversation with a bishop about his royal duty, the upshot of which was that he could never submit to a pagan Dane but must face martyrdom instead. He thinks of his duty as primarily Christian. In whatever way Edmund had actually died, the East Anglians of the next generation knew what to make of him; he fitted into the well-established English class of royal martyr. Alfred did not qualify for this class, though he, too, saw the pagan Danes in much the same light as did Edmund. He, too, was a *rex christianus*, whose kingship was enhanced by fighting pagan foreigners, and as such is represented by Asser, in a biography that is a good deal less secular than Einhard's Charlemagne.[71] The reign of Asser's Alfred is conditioned by the service of God. Indeed, I think Asser's Alfred stands essentially nearer to Alcuin's notion of a king than to Einhard's, despite the use that Asser made of Einhard. He was, according to Asser, a Solomon, a paternal king, careful for all, liberal, just, and intent on learning. None of this distinguishes him from the Carolingians. What does do so is the action he took to ensure the spread of a special kind of learning. It is as an author that he reveals, as no other king, the extent to which the Church had influenced the western concept of kingship.

I wish to look (so far as I am able) at Alfred's concept of kingship in three of his translations: namely, of Gregory's *Cura Pastoralis*, of Orosius, and of Boethius, all of which can be ascribed to Alfred personally.[72] In the first, he faces the problem of how a man in authority should act; in the second, of what God has done in history; and in the third, of what man's

[70] *Memorials of St. Edmund's Abbey*, ed. T. Arnold (Rolls Series, 1890), pp. 8–13.

[71] This is not the place to discuss the 'genuineness' of Asser, to which Professor Whitelock has devoted some convincing pages, *The Genuine Asser* (Stenton Lecture, Reading, 1967). Clearly, however, not all Asser-problems have yet been solved—as, for example, the presence of some Latin usages that need explanation in a ninth-century text.

[72] See Professor Whitelock's authoritative study, 'The prose of Alfred's reign', *Continuations and Beginnings*, ed. E. G. Stanley (1966), pp. 67–103.

relationship is to God. Clearly the Mercian translation of Bede and of Gregory's Dialogues are aspects of the same general interest. Alfred did not select his books for translation with the intention of testing his ideas of kingship; but it was a king who translated, thinking a king's thoughts as he did so; it is a king, in these translations, who reflects on the past and the present; and he thinks through the medium of the books best calculated to reveal what interests him. Why did he choose them and not other books? The answer is, as any acquaintance with ninth-century manuscripts will confirm, that they were the obvious books for his purpose of self-instruction and general instruction in the social role of Christianity. All were familiar in the circle of continental kings and their advisers; that they were not there translated into continental vernaculars is presumably due to the greater knowledge of Latin on the continent than in England, though even so, as Charlemagne bore witness, the need was felt for vernacular explanation if not for translation. Perhaps it is surprising that Augustine's *De Doctrina Christiana* was not among the selected few; the absence of any Isidore, Cassiodorus, and of the *De Civitate Dei* may be explained by their length, by their innate difficulty, or, especially in the last case, by inaccessibility; though there is no clear evidence that they were not available in England. We do not have to assume that any of Alfred's books were specially imported from continental scriptoria; copies may long since have been available in England. The likeliest candidate for special or recent importation would be Boethius, both because of the newly awakened interest in Boethius in Francia and because one of Alfred's learned advisers, Grimbald, came from precisely that circle where Boethian studies were cultivated: he belonged to the confraternity of St. Bertin, Reims, and St. Denis. Doubtless Grimbald brought books with him; one of them, if Mr. Grierson is right,[73] may have been the Prudentius now at Cambridge,[74] with a list of Frankish kings on the first leaf. One could make a case for Prudentius as an

---

[73] 'Grimbald of St. Bertin's', *Engl. Hist. Rev.* lvi (1940), p. 553; but see N. R. Ker, *Catalogue of Manuscripts Containing Anglo-Saxon* (1957), p. 92.

[74] Corpus Christi College, Cambridge, MS. 223; described by M. R. James, *A Descriptive Catalogue of the Manuscripts in the Library of Corpus Christi College, Cambridge*, i (1912), pp. 521–5.

author who might well have interested Alfred; but there is
no reason to believe that this copy was ever meant for him.
Grimbald's influence was deep: to whom, if not to him, can we
ascribe the Frankish entries in the Chronicle? And who would
have been more likely to provide the king with the commentaries
which he, or his advisers, used in translating Boethius and
Orosius? He is Alfred's main, but not only, continental link.

To take Gregory's *Cura Pastoralis* first (as Alfred appears to
have done): the king is translating, and to some extent comment-
ing upon, the book that above all others considers the problems
of one called to fill any *officium* or *ministerium*, specifically in
the Church though not exclusively so. It seems to me that in
Alfred's translation the bishop's office and the king's come
rather closer together than they did in Gregory's text or mind.
In so doing they reflect no view that was exclusively Alfred's
but rather the general outlook of his time; for a king *was* a sort
of bishop, in the sense that he held a sacred office of teaching as
well as of protection within the Christian community. Each,
naturally, had other functions proper to himself alone; but
teaching they had in common, as part of a *ministerium* that
called for training and constant self-examination. In his remarks
to Bishop Werferth that serve as preface to the Worcester manuscript of his translation,[75] Alfred considers the English past: he
looks back to the happy times when kings obeyed God and his
ministers, when they kept peace and order and preserved good
morals at home and enlarged their territories abroad, prospering
in war and in wisdom; it was a time of teaching and learning.[76]
In brief, it was a golden age only in part of the king's imagining,
and a necessary one, such as the Carolingians equally found.
Alfred goes on to say why translations had been unnecessary then
but are necessary now, and adds evidence to show that it is
perfectly respectable for Christian people to make and use translations.[77] Gregory's book is meant primarily for Alfred's bishops;
yet one can see that it is not only the bishop's office that

---

[75] Oxford, Bodl. MS. Hatton 20; see Ker, *Catalogue*, pp. 384 ff., no. 324.
[76] Ed. and trans. by Henry Sweet, *King Alfred's West-Saxon Version of
Gregory's Pastoral Care*, Early English Text Society, o.s. vol. xlv (1871), vol. 1
(1872); see vol. 1, pp. 1–3.
[77] Ibid., p. 6.

he had in mind as he translated: the burden of rule was his as much as theirs, and he is clear that a king, like a bishop, must ask himself if he is fit to rule. Christ had refused to be an earthly king;[78] Saul, anointed (gehalgode) by Samuel, turned from the modesty that made him a suitable candidate, to pride in his own authority;[79] even David, God's darling, was a better man as subject than as king, since as king he murdered Uriah for lust.[80] Yet Alfred is no more willing than Gregory to put the blame on power itself; it is pride and conceit in its possession that brings rulers low.[81] A ruler, then, will not correct his subjects without first weighing up the consequences,[82] but still, in humility, he will be severe when he must be,[83] and excite terror, too.[84] He will have discretion[85] and will constantly correct himself by reading the Scriptures.[86] (One recalls that it was the Psalms that Alfred first learnt,[87] and that he may well have been translating some of the Psalms at the close of his life.)[88] A ruler, however bad he is, must be obeyed by his subjects for fear of God,[89] since to sin against one's lord is to sin against God, who created human authority.[90] In sum, Alfred is content with Gregory's picture of rulers who test and question their own fitness for rule against moral standards but who still, even if they fall short, are entitled to the obedience of their subjects, since their authority is divine. Nor is it without significance that throughout his translation Alfred's word for Christ as Lord is *dryhten*. He sees Christ's lordship in a hierarchical way that has direct application to the kind of society Alfred himself governed; Christians are really God's war-band under Christ's kingship

[78] Ed. and trans. by Henry Sweet, *King Alfred's West-Saxon Version of Gregory's Pastoral Care*, E.E.T.S., see vol. l, p. 33.
[79] Ibid., pp. 35, 112.
[80] Ibid., pp. 392, 35.
[81] Ibid., p. 40.
[82] Ibid., p. 79.
[83] Ibid., p. 106.
[84] Ibid., p. 108.
[85] Ibid., p. 150.
[86] Ibid., p. 168.
[87] Asser, ch. 24, ed. Stevenson, p. 21.
[88] Cf. Whitelock, 'Prose of Alfred's reign', pp. 69, 70, 77; C. and K. Sisam, *The Paris Psalter*, Early English Manuscripts in Facsimile, vol. viii, p. 16.
[89] Sweet, vol. l, p. 196.
[90] Ibid., p. 200.

and that of Christ's deputy, the earthly king.[91] The Carolingians, equally connoisseurs of the *Cura Pastoralis*, drew the same conclusion.

Why Orosius should have appealed to Alfred, and to many of his foreign contemporaries to judge from the surviving manuscripts, is less easy to explain than it appears to be; for Orosius taught, as no other historian, that the past was horrible. It is an over-simplification to state, as is often done, that Orosius painted a gloomy picture of the pagan past in order to highlight the advantages of the Christian present.[92] His picture is subtler: he holds that humanity always did suffer and always will; that the condition of its existence is war, plague, famine, and fire; that the human tragedy can only be seen for what it is if we discard the notion of an ideal and heroic past; that it is people, not periods, that count; and that this is what a true narration of the past must reveal. Responsibility for much of men's suffering rests with their rulers; and this Orosius illustrates from biblical history, drawing the conclusion that people get the rulers they deserve. The difference that Christianity made to the Roman Empire was one of degree: modern wars were no longer for conquest but for justice; the barbarians had been, or would soon be, assimilated; and the Romans could at last embark on their divine mission as spiritual successors to the Israelites. Above all, God's judgement on peoples is revealed in the way that rulers respond to his demands. The historical illustration of this theme is at least as important to Orosius as the proof that the Romans had done better as Christians than ever they did as pagans; for God's judgement had always been operative. Against this Orosian background Alfred may have interpreted Bede, and perhaps also the Anglo-Saxon Chronicle.[93] It can have left him in no doubt that the heroic past was only heroic in so far as kings had served God's purpose; and if he had not accepted this he could scarcely have translated Orosius. It is to the whole of the

---

[91] The point is made by D. H. Green, *The Carolingian Lord*, pp. 326 ff.

[92] See the excellent commentary of B. Lacroix, *Orose et ses idées* (Paris, 1965).

[93] Professor A. Campbell, *The Tollemache Orosius*, Early English Manuscripts in Facsimile, vol. iii, intro., links the three works as forming a continuous historical picture in English eyes. Alfred, however, may not have seen them thus closely related.

work that we should attend, rather than to the characteristic Alfredian additions, if we wish to see why it was important to him as king and teacher of his people. So, as he looks at Orosius's Roman emperors, Alfred shows most interest not in their campaigns but in those personal qualities that revealed a divine purpose; for example, he is more interested in Caesar's clemency and generosity than in his generalship;[94] and what he saw in the Goth Athaulf (though Orosius did not) was a 'most Christian and most clement king'.[95] He makes it a little clearer than Orosius does that all earthly power is kingly, because all such power is derived from the kingship and kingdom of God;[96] and he never loses sight of his own high requirements for a successful king. Regulus, he says (though, again, Orosius does not), told the Romans that he could not be a king of nations since he had once been a slave.[97] In a word, Alfred's Orosius shows how rulers have measured up to God's requirements, whether as Christians or pagans, and how their peoples' prosperity has borne a direct relationship to their success or failure.

But it is in his *Boethius* that Alfred most plainly reveals a kingly purpose.[98] What Boethius wrote was a discourse on the philosophical resources of the public man who has lost everything, and is able, in retrospect, to grasp the irrelevance of riches, offices, friends, and royal favour to the pursuit of happiness. What Alfred writes, under the guise of a translation, is a discourse on the pursuit of happiness through obedience to God's will from the standpoint of a ninth-century king, who, through his advisers, has come to see the matter more as Augustine and Gregory the Great saw it. His approach is theological, not philosophical. Moreover, it is theological in a special sense; for Alfred accepts an interpretation of man's relationship to God that makes room for society as it is, complete with its hierarchies

[94] *King Alfred's Orosius*, ed. H. Sweet, Early English Text Society, o.s. vol. lxxix (1883), pp. 238 ff. Professor Whitelock notes this, 'Prose of Alfred's reign', p. 92.
[95] Trans. of B. Thorpe, *Alfred's Anglo-Saxon Version of Orosius*, appended to R. Pauli, *The Life of Alfred the Great* (1853), p. 512.
[96] Ibid., p. 291.
[97] Ibid., p. 403.
[98] Alfred's *Boethius* has attracted sensible comment from Kurt Otten, *König Alfreds Boethius* (Tübingen, 1964), and Anne Payne, *King Alfred and Boethius* (Wisconsin, 1968).

and its kings. Alfred's *Boethius* is the prime witness to the success of the Church in presenting to the Germanic peoples a theology that took account of their social ideals and made sense of their political organization. Was a Germanic king to be expected to abandon the goods of this world, the pursuit of honour, and the acclaim of friends who saw that he had done well? Not at all.[99] Alfred was not the man to retreat to a monastery, nor is retreat the ideal he holds up to his readers. He prefers action in the present world—the action of every free man to choose the right way to God, whatever the cost; his aim should not be happiness of the Boethian sort in this world but the kingdom of God hereafter. I am uncertain that Alfred fully understood either Boethius's doctrine of divine foreknowledge or his interpretation of eternity;[100] if he did, he rejected both in favour of something more up to date. He prefers the notion of the kingship of God and the personal dependence of every man, but especially the earthly king, upon that kingship. Indeed, Alfred delights in God's overlordship as King of Kings; an overlordship that rests on power, not on love in Boethius's sense.[101] Man is subject to God's power, which does not exhibit itself as predetermined order. Not surprisingly then, Alfred is perfectly clear about the virtue inherent in temporal power, properly exercised under the freedom of choice granted by God as a royal courtesy.[102] Naturally, as Gregory taught, the king's path is a specially hazardous one; he might easily slip into arrogance and greed; in a word, he may cease to be a king and become a tyrant. Alfred has a horror of tyranny, as instanced in his reaction to the murder of their faithful friends by Nero and Antoninus;[103] for it is mere tyranny to betray a follower or a dependant. So far from rejecting worldly goods, a king must use them, as he uses power, in the exercise of his *cræft* or special

[99] I agree with Otten, p. 113, as against Schücking, that Alfred was no more a champion of Christian humility at the expense of honour for good deeds than was Sedulius Scottus, *Liber de rectoribus christianis*, ed. Hellmann, p. 25 (whom, however, Otten slightly misquotes).

[100] I differ here from Anne Payne, *King Alfred*, esp. pp. 49 ff.

[101] Ibid., p. 23.

[102] Ibid., p. 49.

[103] Cf. Otten, pp. 116, 117, who also notes Augustine's and Sedulius's high rating of friendship.

skill (*ministerium*, one may call it); he must know how to use people in their different spheres of activity (as soldiers, for instance, or as priests or labourers). Yet even so he must not expect much in the way of success; it is part of his duty to endure defeat and face death, supported by hope of the kingdom of heaven.[104] Clearly Alfred's *Boethius* is part of his scheme to halt decay in the world he rules, a decay that he believed was illustrated by the assassination of kings and their desertion of their posts.[105] It is conceived for a world very different from that of Boethius, and by a mind that seeks action, not contemplation, which looks for help in a 'wisdom' that was not Boethius's 'philosophy'. His role is that of Solomon, as Charlemagne's had been that of David.[106] Here and there one seems to catch an echo of Pseudo-Cyprian's Twelve Abuses,[107] but fundamentally Alfred's background and approach is that of any king brought up in the theological tradition that stemmed from Augustine. Nothing that he wrote would have struck his Carolingian contemporaries as unorthodox or unkingly; the difference is that he did the writing. We arrive, then, at one firm conclusion from reading Alfred's *Boethius*: it is, that Alfred's God, derived less from barbarian tradition than from Augustine, Gregory, and the commentators, was a king's God, remarkably unlike Boethius's God; and a God that certainly lifted the office of king to a new level.

From Alfred we have something more: not only translation but legislation. Of this Stenton writes that it 'appeared at the end of a century in which no English king had issued laws. Everywhere in western Europe kings were ceasing to exercise the legislative powers which traditionally belonged to their office.'[108] It is a statement of fact, but from it there can be more than one inference. My own would be that Alfred resumed a practice that had been lost in England because he knew that, up to the time of Charles the Bald, the Carolingians had found a use for it. Most of the best surviving manuscripts of continental Germanic law

[104] So Payne, p. 104.
[105] Ibid., pp. 4–5.
[106] Otten, p. 98.
[107] Ibid., p. 116.
[108] *Anglo-Saxon England*, p. 273.

belong to the ninth century, and it was not for nothing that
Charles the Bald had bothered himself with the Theodosian
Code. To assemble the *Volksrechte* and reissue them as their
own had seemed an enhancement of kingship to the Carolingians;[109] it was a legislative function with political overtones.
Alfred, however, did more than this. To revise and reissue his
predecessors' laws as his own was nothing new; but his remarkable prologue suggests something else. 'The only object of this
introduction', in Stenton's view, 'was to acquaint his subjects with
what Alfred regarded as a piece of model legislation.'[110] Certainly
it was one object, and it implies another: to link his own legislation with that of the Bible, and by linking it to accept the Bible
as valid moral law. With modifications he accepts the Mosaic
law of Exodus as current, and by an excerpt from St. Matthew
he demonstrates that Christ had also accepted it as current and
valid. The righteous man, says Alfred, needs no other law-
book;[111] the ethic of the Decalogue was an acceptable basis for
all law.[112] But men were not righteous; they did need other law;
and Alfred shows how, since the critical event of the baptism
of Æthelberht, such law had been provided for the English
people. He in his turn does what he can: the collection of laws
that he makes for them is what he would probably have called
Christian law. We have seen how much he relied on that law
in the interpretation of his own office. What is much less clear
than in the case of his contemporaries abroad is the extent to
which he relied on the Church for that interpretation. Unlike
the Carolingians he was short of bishops: he had no Hincmar.
His relations with the bishops of his entourage seem mostly to
have been confined to matters of learning and teaching; that is,
as far as the evidence goes. Yet there are slight indications that
he thought he owed his bishops obedience. A letter from Pope
John VIII to Archbishop Ethelred in 877 or 878 reveals that the
king had had an admonitory letter from Rome and had been

---

[109] See Wattenbach-Levison, *Deutschlands Geschichtsquellen im Mittelalter*,
Beiheft: R. Buchner, *Die Rechtsquellen* (Weimar, 1953).
[110] *Anglo-Saxon England*, p. 273. This prologue is, as Professor Whitelock
shows ('Prose of Alfred's reign', p. 96), 'carefully thought-out'.
[111] Liebermann, *Gesetze*, i. 44 (prol., 49, 6).
[112] Ibid. iii, pp. 32–5.

told to obey his archbishop.[113] Moreover, the tone of the correspondence of Archbishop Fulk of Reims with the king suggests that he could be relied on to accept episcopal guidance in moral matters, as well perhaps as in church appointments.[114] Fulk's tone may indeed be 'arrogant and patronizing', but it was precisely that to which even the most formidable Carolingians were accustomed. Moreover, Alfred had turned to the Church of the mighty St. Remigius of Reims as a suppliant; an important part of his own programme of reform would turn on the response of its archbishop; and he would expect, and even wish, paternal advice. He does not seem to have resented it, at any rate.

I have said nothing of the disputed matter of Alfred's unction. We do not know that he was anointed at his accession nor that he ever indulged in festal *coronamenta* like the Carolingians. The Chronicle, in a much-disputed passage under the year 853, records that as a child Alfred was consecrated king in Rome by the pope; yet this is not what the pope told King Æthelwulf in a letter written soon after: he says that the boy was invested as consul.[115] It has always seemed a stumbling-block that Alfred should not have known and remembered what happened to him in Rome;[116] and a case, though not a very good one, can be made for his having in fact been consecrated king.[117] It would not be surprising if the clergy, such as there were, had participated in his inauguration in 871; but there is no evidence that they did. What perhaps is most significant is the lack of evidence: consecration, if it happened, did not strike his English contemporaries as the source of his royal power, still less as a weapon by which the Church could control him. And it did not strike Alfred, either. It may be that we attach the wrong sort of importance to ninth-century royal unction. It is susceptible of so many interpretations. In so far as it was an inauguration ceremony, it reflected the belief of the king that it helped him; but

---

[113] *MGH Epist. Karo Aevi*, v, no. 75, pp. 71 ff. Professor Whitelock, *English Historical Documents*, c. *500–1042* (1955), p. 811, doubts whether the pope's letter to the king ever reached him. Clearly the pope thought it had.

[114] Birch, *Cart. Sax.* ii, no. 555 (recte 556), p. 190.

[115] *MGH Epist. Karo. Aevi*, iii, p. 602, no. 31.

[116] Cf. Whitelock, *Anglo-Saxon Chronicle*, pp. xxii, xxiii. Dr. Janet Nelson has examined the matter at some length in her thesis, pp. 398 ff.

[117] John, *Orbis Britanniae*, pp. 38 ff.

it is another matter to claim that without it he would have been no king. Alfred's assurance of the divine origin of his kingship and his resolve to interpret it in the light of Christian doctrine had no apparent connection with unction. He was a king as the Carolingians were kings: by inheritance and by evident signs of divine approval. There may be no more to it than that.

It will not be disputed that kingship, where I must leave it in the ninth century, is extremely unlike kingship, in so far as we see it at all, in the fourth and fifth centuries; and the difference is not of size merely. It has been transformed into an office with duties and rights defined by churchmen. We cannot tell precisely how far kings themselves were conscious of the transformation. Should we now call kingship Christian rather than Germanic? I think that it is still Germanic; warfare still holds a prime place in western society: it is still a way of life as much as a means of survival or expansion. It is the tasks of peace that have undergone change. Still kings look back; more so, perhaps; genealogies, legends, and history are part of their stock-in-trade, and those who provide this national past are the same men who also proffer a biblical past for inspection and imitation by kings. Offa, Alcuin, and Charlemagne, Hincmar, Charles the Bald, and Alfred, all look back. The greatest of them, Bede, looked back to greatest effect. His History was the most successful of the post-Gregorian attempts to construct a literary past for a Germanic people ruled by kings; in effect, a mirror of princes of unexampled power.

INDEX

Aachen (*see also* palace school), 109
Abbo of Fleury, 141
Abingdon, monastery of, 90
accession, royal, 55
Achish, 77 ff.
acta, Charles the Bald's, 126 ff.
acta martyrum, 51
acta, Paris, 137
Adaloald, Lombardic king, 30
Adam of Bremen, 12
admonitio generalis of 789, 107 ff.
admonitio of 823–5, 136 ff.
Adomnan, 57, 94
aequitas, 48
Ælfflaed, abbess, 61, 82, 91
Ælfthryth, abbess, 60
Ælfwald, East Anglian king, 60
Ælfwald, Northumbrian king, 119
Æthelbald, Mercian king, 61, 110, 113
Æthelberg, abbess of Faremoutiers, 91
Æthelberht, Kentish king, chap. II *passim*, 67, 80, 149
Æthelfrith, Northumbrian king, 78
Æthelred, Mercian king, 90
Æthelred, Northumbrian king, 116, 118, 119
Æthelthryth, Northumbrian queen, 63, 65, 79 n., 91
Æthelwald, Northumbrian king, 94
Æthelwulf, West Saxon king, 134, 140, 150
Africa, 12
Agatho, pope, 68 ff.
Ahab, king, 75, 125
Aidan, king of Dal-Réti, 57 ff.
Aidan, St., 85 ff.
Alamans, 19
Albinus, abbot, 78
Alcuin, 56, 87, 88, 95, 100 ff., 114, 116, 117 ff., 123, 128, 138, 141
Aldfrith, Northumbrian king, 62, 64, 69
Aldhelm, St., 89, 90
Aldwulf, East Anglian king, 60

Alfred, West Saxon king, chap. VI *passim*, 35, 74, 80
Alhfrith, Deiran sub-king, 63, 94, 96
Amalasuntha, Ostrogothic queen, 92
Amand, St., 58 ff.
amicitia, 101, 109
Ammianus Marcellinus, 15
amor, 138
Angel, kings of, 112
Anna, East Anglian king, 85
annales Regni Francorum, 129
annalists, 109
annals, 117
antiqua, Visigothic, 34
Antoninus, emperor, 147
apostacy, 44
Aquitaine, 133 ff., 134 n., 135 ff.
Arabs (Muslims), 98, 103
Arianism, 9, 27, 29, 30, 44, 79
Ariovistus, 5
Arles, 38
Arminius, 6
Arnulf, St., bishop of Metz, 131
assassination, royal, 115
Asser, 116, 141
Athaulf, Gothic king, 146
Athelstan, West Saxon king, 96
Attigny, penance of, 124
auctoritas, 120
Augustine, St., archbishop of Canterbury, 25, 29, 30, 31, 32, 38, 40
Augustine, St., bishop of Hippo, 30, 73, 104, 122, 138, 142, 148
Augustine's Oak, St., conference at, 31
Aunegundis, Merovingian queen, 50
Aurelius Caninus, 75
Autun, 38
Avars, 103, 116

Balthildis, Merovingian queen, 52, 92
Bamburgh, 84
Bapchild, 66
Bardney, monastery of, 82, 84, 91

corrector, 107
Coulaines, treaty of, 125 ff.
court poets, 106
cræft, 147
crusaders, Carolingians as, 138
Cummean, 69
Cuneglas, 75
Cura Pastoralis, 143 ff.
Cuthbert, St., 59, 61 ff., 88, 94, 96
Cwichelm, West Saxon king, 80

Dagobert I, Merovingian king, 48, 52
Dagobert II, Merovingian king, 52
Daniel, bishop of Winchester, 90
David, king, 48, 49, 53, 63, 71, 77 ff., 96, 101, 103, 125, 129, 130, 133 n., 136, 137, 138, 144, 148
de duodecim abusivis saeculi, see Pseudo-Cyprian
defensio, 126, 137, 139
de institutione regia, 137
deliberatio, 49
deposition of kings, 134
de regis persona, 139
Desiderius, bishop of Vienne, Life of, 51
Diadema Monachorum, 136
Dietrich of Bern, 9
disputatio de rhetorica, 101
disticha Catonis, 3
doctor, 101
dominus terrae, 139
domus regis, 131
Drida, 116
dryhten, 144
Dryhthelm, 94
duces, early Germanic, chap. I *passim*
Dunnichen Moss (Nechtansmere), battle of, 62
dux, 15, 101

Eadbald, Kentish king, 92 n.
Eadburh, daughter of Offa, 116
Eadwulf, Northumbrian king, 64
Eanfflaed, abbess, 63, 82, 86, 91
Eanfrid, Northumbrian king, 93
Eardwulf, Northumbrian king, 117, 118, 120
East Angles, 111
East Germans, 9

Ebroin, Frankish mayor of palace, 81
Ecgberht, bishop of York, 91
Ecgburgh, abbess, 60
Ecgfrith, Mercian king, 112, 114, 118, 119
Ecgfrith, Northumbrian king, 61, 62, 64, 94
edicts, royal Frankish, 36 n.
Edington, battle of, 140
Edmund, East Anglian king, 141
Edwin, Northumbrian king, 80, 81, 82, 87
Egbert, West Saxon king, 116, 117, 140
Einhard, 50, 102, 108, 109, 115, 123, 128 ff., 141
emendatio, 119
emperors, Eastern, 114
Ennodius, 9
Eorconberht, Kentish king, 28, 63
Eorcongota, Kentish princess, 91
Eormenric, Kentish king, 38
Eriugena, John Scotus, 132
Ermoldus Nigellus, 136
eruditio, 101
Ethelred, archbishop of Canterbury, 149
Eulogius, patriarch of Alexandria, 28 n.
Euric, Visigothic king, 33 ff.
Eusebius, 72
Euthiones, 24, 25
exempla Romanorum, 33 ff., 37

felicitas, 73, 95, 102
feud, 35, 41 ff., 64, 107 ff.
fidelitas, 107
Finglesham, 27
Finnsburh, 121
fiscus, 65
fortuna, 109
forum judicum, 55
Frankfurt, synod of, 103 ,118 ff.
Frankish kingship, origins of, 17
Franks, 16 ff., 23 ff.
Franks casket, 71 n.
Fredegar, 17, 18, 48, 51, 75, 99
Frey, 8, 12
Frisians, 25
Frithuwold, sub-king of Surrey, 66
Fulgentius, 79

PRINTED IN GREAT BRITAIN
AT THE UNIVERSITY PRESS, OXFORD
BY VIVIAN RIDLER
PRINTER TO THE UNIVERSITY